ISTANBUL

ISTANBUL

Recipes from the heart of Turkey

REBECCA SEAL

PHOTOGRAPHY BY
STEVEN JOYCE

hardie grant books
MELBOURNE · LONDON

For our parents
Dave, Hilary, Patrick and Sheila

Introduction

No matter how many times I visit, Istanbul remains a fascinating place. A city of 17 million people covering 2000 square miles and straddling the border between Asia and Europe, it is an incredible mixture of the very old – traces of Neolithic settlements were recently discovered near the Old Town, Sultanahmet – and the very new, as shiny modern towers leap up next to domed mosques or stone churches.

Istanbul's food culture is as diverse as its architecture, with influences coming from the Persians and Ottomans of the past; its Middle Eastern neighbours, the Greeks, Armenians, Turks and Kurds; nearby Asian and European countries; and Christian, Orthodox, Muslim and Jewish communities. The result is a riot of tastes, in dishes cooked using the best of local and seasonal ingredients from both the surrounding countryside and the sea.

Whenever I visit Istanbul and start to ask questions about Turkish food, someone always reminds me that it doesn't really make sense to talk about 'Turkish' food as every dish is connected to the specific place it came from. A particular meal may be made different ways in different streets in the same neighbourhood, depending on where the cook or the cook's family come from. Like the Turkish language, food is seen as a carrier of culture. What each community here shares, however, is a love of strong flavours – whether it's the heat of spice, the tang of salty pickles or the sticky sweetness of honey.

Food is at the centre of everything here, whether in upmarket areas like old-money Nişantaşı, where you're perhaps more likely to catch a whiff of truffles than charcoal-grilled meats, or on the waterfront at Galata Bridge buying a fish sandwich and beer taken from a bucket of ice.

Celebrations and meals out usually start with a selection of meze dishes, some hot and some cold, for everyone to share. Many restaurants don't have menus, but instead bring round huge trays laden with mezes for you to pick from, or beckon you to choose from the counter. They can be anything from dishes of pickles and dips to fried vegetables, salads, cheeses, fish, meat and poultry dishes. Meze are not meant to be rushed – have two or three per person, plus some breads for scooping, and nibble them alongside some excellent Turkish wine, a cold glass of aniseed raki or a Turkish beer.

Elinize sağlık! Afiyet olsun! (Health to your hands! Enjoy the food!)

REBECCA SEAL

Key ingredients

There are a few ingredients that make all the difference to Turkish cooking. Although there are good alternatives that you can use if you can't get hold of them, they are all easy to order online and some of them you can find in supermarkets. In fact, once my obsession with Turkey's food really took hold, I discovered four Turkish stores within a short distance of my house on the outskirts of London. Ask around in your neighbourhood – they might look like newsagents or convenience stores, but all you need is a couple of shelves of Turkish goodies in the back and you're all set.

Turkish Tomato Paste (Domates Salçası)
Turkish tomato paste is a very concentrated paste of slowly cooked tomatoes with salt. In some dishes – ones that will be cooked for a long time – you can substitute regular concentrated tomato purée (paste) for Turkish tomato paste. But in anything uncooked, it's best to leave it out or substitute a finely diced, deseeded fresh tomato or two. You'll lose the bright red colour the paste lends to dishes like *Kısır* (page 204) but there are so many other great flavours in it that it won't matter too much (and tomato purée would spoil it). Italian sun-dried tomato purée is a fair substitute in uncooked dishes, although make sure it's not full of extra herbs. You can buy the most enormous jars of Turkish tomato paste and they will keep for weeks once opened, in the fridge, as long as you pour a layer of vegetable oil over the exposed top to prevent the air getting to it. Or freeze it in small portions (an ice cube tray is a good idea). Some brands can be salty, so taste the dish you've added it to before adding more seasoning.

Red Pepper Paste (Biber Salçası)
This can be mild or hot – make sure you check because hot really means hot! It keeps better than tomato paste and lends a lovely rich flavour to everything from salads to lamb dishes. Pour a layer of vegetable oil over the top to help it keep longer in the fridge. You can find it online or in Turkish or Middle Eastern stores. See page 214 for a recipe for a quick homemade red pepper paste. As with tomato paste, red pepper paste can be salty, so taste for seasoning before adding salt to your dish.

Pomegranate Molasses

You can get this in lots of supermarkets and it keeps forever so it's worth having a bottle in the cupboard – you can use it in recipes from all over the region, not just Turkish-inspired dishes. If you can't get hold of any, lemon juice is a good match for its sourness or a little splash of balsamic vinegar will add its sweet sharpness and brown colour. It's used in salad dressings, especially with bulghur wheat, and for marinading.

Pul Biber (Red Pepper Flakes)

This is scattered over food in Istanbul like we grind black pepper. It can vary from spicy to mild and, once you've tried it, you'll be as addicted as I am. The bright red flakes are found in little bowls on most meal tables and they have a distinctively different taste to the kind of chilli flakes we might scatter over pizza or into chilli con carne. You can buy bags of pul biber very cheaply online or in Turkish stores. You can use other dried mild chilli flakes but the flavour won't be the same.

Sumac

Sumac is a dark red spice with a zesty, citrussy flavour. Again, it is easy to get in some supermarkets, Middle Eastern stores and online. Sumac is sprinkled over finely sliced raw onions, a traditional accompaniment to grilled kebabs or meats like liver. You'll also see it scattered over salads, used to flavour chicken and fish, or in meatballs. You can add a little lemon juice if you don't have sumac to hand.

Recipe notes

- Onions are large white onions, unless otherwise stated

- All vegetables are medium-sized unless otherwise stated

- Eggs are medium-sized, fresh and free-range, unless otherwise stated

- Olive oil is extra-virgin olive oil, unless otherwise stated

- For the fish recipes I recommend that you buy your fish from
  sustainable fisheries

- When I give two figures in the number of people a recipe will serve,
  the smaller one is if serving as a main course, the larger one is if serving
  as a meze dish

- This book gives metric and imperial equivalent measures:
  for best results stick to one or other in a recipe. It also uses metric cup
  measurements (i.e. 250 ml/8½ fl oz for 1 cup); please note that a US cup
  is 225 ml (8 fl oz), slightly smaller than a metric cup, so check before use
  and, if using these, be generous in your cup measurements

  1 teaspoon = 5 ml
  1 tablespoon = 15 ml
  1 cup = 250 ml

KAHVALTI

Breakfast

Traditionally, most Turkish people would just eat freshly baked bread, cheese and olives for breakfast. In Istanbul however, there are lots of ways to start the day – from spicy scrambled eggs to a water-melon and cheese salad. If breakfast blurs into brunch, try starting the day with a hearty lentil soup or *gözleme*, hot pastry parcels filled with melting cheese and herbs.

Menemen

Spiced Scrambled Eggs

This is great with slices of *sucuk*, rich grilled beef sausage, but you could also have it with chorizo or other spicy sausage. It's a perfect brunch or light vegetarian supper, on its own with warm flatbreads or toast.

SERVES 2
knob of butter
1 small, long green pepper, finely chopped (or ½ green (bell) pepper)
2 spring onions (scallions), finely chopped
1 large fresh tomato, deseeded and finely chopped
2 teaspoons Turkish tomato paste or tomato purée
1 teaspoon Turkish red pepper paste (page 214)
4 eggs, lightly beaten
40 g (1½ oz/¼ cup) crumbled feta
1 tablespoon finely chopped flat-leaf parsley
pul biber or mild chilli flakes
flatbreads, pieces of baguette or crusty white bread to serve

Melt the butter in a pan big enough to take all the ingredients and gently fry the pepper and onion for 2 minutes, stirring. Add the chopped tomato and cook gently for 5 minutes.

Add the tomato and pepper paste, plus a tablespoon of water to loosen the mixture, if your fresh tomato is not very juicy. Cook for 2 minutes, stirring to blend, then pour in the beaten eggs. Stir gently and, as they start to scramble, add the crumbled feta, parsley and chilli flakes (you probably won't need any salt as feta is quite salty).

Continue stirring gently to blend the eggs with the tomato. When the eggs are scrambled to your liking, remove from the heat and serve with flatbreads, pieces of baguette or crusty white bread.

Karpuz Salatası

Watermelon, Mint, Olive and Cheese Salad

This is a lovely zingy dish to start the day. You could use hard or soft goat's cheese instead of feta (which I use because it's easier to find than *beyaz peynir*, the Turkish equivalent), or different kinds of melon. For added richness, drizzle the salad with a little good-quality olive oil.

SERVES 4

200 g (7 oz) feta, cut into 2 cm (¾ in) cubes
½ watermelon, rind and seeds removed and cut into 2.5 cm (1 in) cubes
large handful of mint leaves, roughly torn
24 stoned black olives
freshly squeezed lemon juice to taste

Mix all the ingredients except the lemon juice together. Taste and add lemon juice a little at a time – you want to balance the melon's sweetness, so how much you need depends on its ripeness.

Cılbır

Poached Egg in Garlic Yoghurt

This dish is a Turkish breakfast favourite. It sounds like a strange combination but works brilliantly. It's easy to increase the quantities to feed more people – just poach your eggs until they are almost ready (1–2 minutes), gently transfer them to a bowl of iced water until you're ready to serve, then reheat in boiling water for 30 seconds. Be sure to use the freshest eggs available, otherwise they'll disintegrate into long trailing strands in the pan. If you have time, bring the yoghurt up to room temperature, as otherwise there will be a big contrast between the cold sauce and the hot egg. If you find your paprika a bit insipid, experiment with Spanish smoked paprika. It's not at all authentically Turkish, but it is much more delicious than the low-quality regular paprika sold in some supermarkets.

SERVES 1

75 ml (2½ fl oz/generous ¼ cup) plain Turkish or Greek-style yoghurt
½–1 garlic clove to taste, crushed
salt to taste
15 g (½ oz/1 tablespoon) butter
1 egg
½ teaspoon lemon juice
1 teaspoon sweet paprika
chopped dill or flat-leaf parsley for sprinkling (optional)
freshly ground black pepper (optional)
pul biber or mild chilli flakes for sprinkling (optional)
flatbread, baguette or white sourdough bread for dipping

Mix the yoghurt in a bowl with the garlic and a little salt, to taste. Transfer it to a bowl large enough to take the yoghurt sauce and a poached egg. Poach the egg to your liking in simmering water with the lemon juice added – I cook mine for 3 minutes maximum, over a low heat.

While the eggs are poaching melt the butter, in a pan over a very low heat. As soon as it starts to sizzle take it off the heat. Wait a moment before adding the paprika to the butter – if the spice burns it will taste bitter. When the egg is done, lift it gently from the water with a slotted spoon, allow it to drain and then slide it into the bowl so it nestles in the yoghurt.

Drizzle with the bright red melted butter and scatter over the herbs and black pepper and chilli flakes, if using. Serve with a flatbread, a piece of baguette or a chunky slice of white sourdough bread, for dipping in the yolk and yoghurt.

Ezo Gelin Çorbası

Ezo-the-Bride's Red Lentil Soup

This soup is named after a real person: Ezo was a very beautiful woman born in the early twentieth century who was unhappily married. She tried to make her mother-in-law like her by making her this soup. Her story and the recipe spread all over Turkey, and today Ezo's soup is eaten for breakfast or as part of a main meal. I like it as part of a hearty weekend brunch.

SERVES 4

1 garlic clove, finely chopped
1 onion, finely chopped
20 g (¾ oz/1½ tablespoons) butter
3 tablespoons Turkish tomato paste or concentrated tomato
  purée (paste)
1 teaspoon sweet paprika
200 g (7 oz/generous ¾ cup) red lentils, picked over and rinsed
3 tablespoons fine burghul (bulgur) wheat (optional)
1.2 litres (40 fl oz/5 cups) chicken or vegetable stock
salt and freshly ground black pepper
1 tablespoon dried mint (or less to taste) to serve
chilli flakes to serve
lemon wedges to serve

Slowly soften the garlic and onion in the butter over a low heat until translucent. Add the tomato paste and paprika and cook for 2 minutes, stirring. Then add the lentils, burghul (if using) and stock. Bring to the boil and simmer for 30 minutes, stirring occasionally to prevent sticking.

Once the lentils are soft and beginning to fall apart, take off the heat and blitz in a blender until fairly smooth. Taste for seasoning and add salt and pepper if necessary. Serve sprinkled with a light dusting of dried mint, chilli flakes and a squeeze of lemon.

Gözleme

Fried Cheese Parcels

If you spy a woman sitting in the window of a café in Istanbul, wearing white and rolling circles of pastry out very thinly, stuffing, folding and cooking them on what looks like an upturned wok, the chances are she's making *gözleme*, a stuffed and pan-fried street food snack. Often the pastry is folded into a large crescent shape around the filling, before being cooked on a rounded grill called a sac, then rolled up to serve, wrapped in paper. You can also fold gözleme into squares like envelopes before cooking, or serve it in slices for breakfast, which I like to do. They are very flat pastries, so don't over-stuff them.

MAKES 4
For the dough:
300 g (10½ oz/scant 2½ cups) plain (all-purpose) flour, plus extra
    for dusting
1 teaspoon salt

For the filling:
200 g (7 oz) halloumi (or hard mozzarella or cheddar)
1 small fresh red chilli, deseeded and finely chopped (or less to taste)
1 tablespoon finely chopped flat-leaf parsley

30 g (1 oz/2 tablespoons) butter, melted for brushing

Mix together the dough ingredients with about 200 ml (7 fl oz/generous ¾ cup) water, to form a sticky dough (you may not need all the water). Knead for 10 minutes then place in a bowl and cover with a damp cloth or clingfilm (plastic wrap). Set aside for 20 minutes.

Meanwhile, prepare the filling. Finely chop or grate the cheese and mix with the remaining ingredients. Put your largest frying pan over a high heat.

Divide the dough into quarters and on a floured work surface with a floured rolling pin, roll one out into a circle about 30 cm (12 in) diameter and about 3 mm (⅛ in) thick. If your frying pan is smaller than this then make 6 or 8 smaller gözleme. Scatter a quarter of the filling evenly over the bottom half of the semi-circle and lightly wet the edges. Fold the top half over the bottom half to make a half-moon shape and press to seal the pastry edges.

Using a large spatula, carefully slide the sealed gözleme into the hot pan. Cook for 3–4 minutes, until little brown spots appear on the underside, then flip over. Brush the cooked top with a little melted butter. When the other side is covered with little golden-brown flecks too, and the pastry no longer appears damp or raw, again about 3 minutes, slide the gözleme out of the pan and keep warm while you make the rest.

COOK'S TIP
Try these fillings. Quantities aren't important but not too much as the pastries must be flattish once stuffed (so only around 225 g/8 oz total prepared weight):

- A handful of fresh spinach with crumbled feta
- A little cooked and finely chopped potato, sweet potato or squash, with softened onion, fresh herbs and/or cheese
- Softened sliced leeks with dill
- Goat's cheese and parsley
- Finely sliced mushrooms with spinach and toasted pine nuts (pine kernels)
- Cooked spiced lamb or beef mince (ground beef)
- Cooked spicy sausage with cheese

Ballı Yoğurt

Yoghurt, Fruit and Honey

In Istanbul, every now and then you'll come across a little store specialising in delicious Turkish honey, with huge gold jars gleaming on the shelves, honeycomb suspended in the amber liquid. Often they will also sell fresh creamy Turkish yoghurt from the counter in front. A cup of this, drizzled with intensely floral honey, makes a wonderful simple breakfast for commuters on the way to work. At home, I like to add a handful of nuts and seasonal fruit (the quantities don't matter, it's according to taste), a squeeze of lemon and a few torn mint leaves, as well. In the winter, swap fresh fruit for dried fruits (figs, berries or apple), *kuru yemiş* in Turkish, which are sold loose from teetering pyramids on market stalls all over the city.

SERVES 1

handful of fresh fruit, cut into bite-sized pieces: figs, melon, apple, pear, grapes, pomegranate, plums, peaches, or a little less of dried fruit

3-4 mint leaves, roughly torn (optional)

75 ml (2½ fl oz/generous ¼ cup) plain Turkish or Greek-style yoghurt

freshly squeezed lemon juice to taste

2 tablespoons clear honey

small handful of unsalted pistachios, hazelnuts or flaked almonds, or a mixture of all three

Place the fresh or dried fruit in a serving bowl or cup and scatter over the mint, if using. Spoon the yoghurt over the fruit and squeeze over a little lemon juice. Drizzle the honey on top and then scatter over the nuts. Eat straight away.

İncir Reçeli

Fig Jam

This jam is delicious with *kaymak*, a Turkish clotted cream made with buffalo milk. Fortunately, since it's pretty hard to get kaymak outside Turkey, it's also wonderful with regular clotted cream, or smeared onto hot toast with butter.

MAKES 2 JARS, about 700 g (1½ lb)
450 g (1 lb) ripe figs
juice of 1 lemon
225 g (8 oz/1 cup) granulated or preserving sugar

Wash 2 jam jars and their lids, then let them dry in a low oven for about half an hour, to sterilise. Meanwhile, trim the tops off the figs and then slice each fig into 8 segments. Then chop each segment into 2 or 3 pieces.

Heat 250 ml (8½ fl oz/1 cup) water, lemon juice and sugar together in a stainless steel or preserving pan, stirring, until the sugar has dissolved then bring to a simmer.

Add the figs to the pan and simmer gently until the fruit is pulpy, about 30 minutes. If you don't like seeds in your jam, skim them off with a shallow spoon as they rise to the surface (you could also sieve or strain them out).

When the fruit has broken down, check to see if the jam has reached setting point. If you have a sugar thermometer, it needs to boil for 10 minutes to 105°C (221°F). If you don't have one, put a plate in the freezer. When it has chilled, place a drop of jam onto the plate – if it slightly sets and wrinkles when you tilt the plate, then the jam has reached setting point. Pour into the warm sterilised jars. Seal with a lid immediately and allow to cool. Store in the fridge and eat within a couple of weeks.

PİDELER VE HAMUR İŞLERI

Breads and Savoury Pastries

In Istanbul you are never far from a bakery. Wherever you are in the city, there will be a neighbourhood store close by, and people visit two or three times a day so as to have fresh, warm bread with every meal. As well as bread, Turkish cooks make wonderful versions of pizza, *lahmacun* and *pide*, one thin and one softer and thick, topped with spiced meat, buttery melted cheese or *sucuk* sausage.

Lavaş

Flatbreads

Bread is a very important part of a Turkish meal and these flatbreads are both tasty and versatile. In Istanbul they can look a little less flat: some restaurants take great pride in turning them into balloon breads, displaying freshly made, puffed up lavaş by the doors. (I also once saw one taped to the wall of a restaurant, which I suspect was a little less fresh …) Use lavaş as wraps or cut them into wedges for scooping up dips or mopping up sauces. You can also cook these on the barbecue, giving them a lovely smoky taste. Once the flames have died down and the coals are white, place the breads directly onto the metal rack – keep an eye on them as they may cook very quickly if the coals are very hot.

MAKES 16
350 ml (12 fl oz/1⅓ cups) lukewarm water
1 tablespoon active dried yeast
1 tablespoon caster (superfine) sugar
2 tablespoons olive oil
500 g (1 lb 2 oz/4 cups) strong white bread flour
2 teaspoons salt

Mix the water, yeast, sugar and oil together in a jug. Leave in a warm place for 10–15 minutes to activate the yeast. It should form a thick, frothy head.

In a large mixing bowl, add the yeast mixture to the flour and salt and mix thoroughly. The dough will be fairly sticky at this stage. On a floured surface, knead the dough for 10 minutes, using floured hands and knuckles to stretch the dough out, before folding it back on itself until smooth and elastic. (If it is really too sticky to do this, add a tablespoon or two of flour to the mix.)

Place the dough in an oiled bowl, cover with a damp cloth or oiled cling-film (plastic wrap) and leave in a warm place for about an hour or until doubled in size. (Depending on the temperature, it may take longer to double in size. You can tell when it has finished rising as the dough will dent rather than spring back when you press it.)

Knock back the risen dough. Divide in half, and then continue dividing it until you have 16 little balls of dough. On a floured surface and using a floured rolling pin, roll the dough out into circles about 20 cm (8 in) in diameter and about 5 mm (¼ in) thick. If you want bigger lavaş, stop when you've divided the dough into 8 pieces and roll them to about 30 cm (12 in) in diameter.

Heat a large frying pan over a high heat (don't add any oil). Cook the lavaş on one side until the dough bubbles and begins to brown, just 1 or 2 minutes, and then flip over. Once the other side has started to brown, remove from the pan and keep warm while cooking the remainder. They should still be floppy enough to fold or roll into a wrap. If you accidentally overcook the lavaş, put in a plastic box with a lid and allow to steam slightly to soften, or mist with water. Before cooking the next lavaş, wipe any specks of flour out of the pan with a sheet of paper towel, as they will burn and stick to the next flatbread you cook. Repeat until all the lavaş are made.

Yalanci Lavaş

Cheat's Lavaş

When short of time, I make this version of lavaş. It's not quite as tasty, but takes just a few minutes to rustle up. Try and use good-quality flour as it will taste better.

MAKES 16
350 ml (12 fl oz/ 1⅓ cups) lukewarm water
500g (1 lb 2 oz/4 cups) plain (all-purpose) white flour
2 teaspoons salt

Mix the ingredients together to form a fairly sticky dough. On a floured surface and with floured hands, knead the dough for 10 minutes, by which time it will be stretchy, elastic and much less sticky. Put in a bowl, cover with a damp cloth or clingfilm (plastic wrap) and leave to stand for 20 minutes, then knead again.

Divide into 16 balls and roll out into discs no more than 5 mm (¼ in) thick. Heat a large frying pan over a high heat (don't add any oil). Cook the lavaş as on the previous page until bubbled and brown all over but still floppy enough to fold and roll.

Pide

Pide with Cheese and Sausage

These rich, canoe-shaped stuffed breads make a perfect weekend brunch or supper. In Istanbul they are served with lots of different toppings, like spiced minced (ground) meat (you could use the topping from the lahmacun recipe on page 46), kasseri cheese and tomato, grilled (bell) peppers, sausage or egg – and are almost always washed down with a glass of salty ayran (page 243).

Simsek Pide, just off Taksim Square and next to the French Consulate is a great place for authentic pide, with crisp crusts and just the right amount of melted, buttery cheese.

MAKES 4
For the dough:
175 ml (6 fl oz/¾ cup) milk
1 tablespoon active dried yeast
1 tablespoon sugar
1 tablespoon olive oil
250 g (9 oz/2 cups) strong white bread flour
½ teaspoon salt
a little polenta, cornmeal or semolina (cream of wheat) for dusting

For the filling:
200 g (7 oz/2 cups) grated hard cheese – I use a mixture of cheddar and hard mozzarella
1 or 2 *sucuk* sausages, finely sliced (or use chorizo or pepperoni)

Warm the milk slightly until lukewarm. Mix it with the yeast, sugar and oil in a jug and leave for 10–15 minutes to activate the yeast. It should form a thick, frothy head.

In a bowl, mix the liquid with the flour and salt, working it with your hands to create a soft, sticky dough. With floured hands, knead the dough for 10 minutes until smooth and elastic: if it is very wet you may need to start doing this in the bowl first before turning it out onto a floured surface. Wipe a little oil around the inside of a clean bowl. Place the dough in the bowl, cover it with a damp cloth or oiled clingfilm (plastic wrap) and leave in a warm place to rise for about an hour or until it has doubled in size. (Depending on the temperature, it may take longer to double in size. You can tell when it has finished rising as the dough will dent rather than spring back when you press it.)

Meanwhile, preheat the oven to 230°C (450°F/gas 9) and put two pizza stones or upturned large baking trays in to heat up. Knock back the dough to almost its original size. Divide into 4 balls and set aside to rest for 15 minutes.

Have ready four pieces of baking paper, about 40 × 20 cm (16 × 8 in). Dust each one with a little flour, polenta, cornmeal or semolina. Roll out each ball into a narrow oblong on a floured surface with a floured pin to roughly 30 × 10 cm (12 × 4 in). Slide each piece of dough onto a prepared sheet of baking paper.

Scatter a quarter of the cheese along the middle of each piece of dough. Wet the ends of the dough ovals and pinch them together and upwards, like prow of a boat. Fold the sides inwards, creating a 1 cm (½ in) lip all the way around the pide. This will enclose the cheese (or other filling) and stop it running out when it melts. Arrange 5 or 6 slices of sucuk or other sausage on each pide.

Take the hot stones or baking trays out of the oven and slide the paper sheets and the dough on to them (cook in two batches if necessary). Bake the pide for 7–8 minutes, until the dough has puffed up and browned, the cheese has melted and is bubbling and the sausage is sizzling. Serve immediately, either whole or sliced into small slivers.

Lahmacun

Traditional Lahmacun

In Istanbul, lahmacun, a Turkish alternative to pizza, come in many forms: some are baked so the dough is crisp and crunchy, others are so soft they are served rolled up and wrapped in paper. Traditionally they are topped with spiced lamb, then finished with a squeeze of lemon. It is impossible to get authentic blackened and bubbled crusts in a domestic oven, but if you crank it up to its maximum heat you can achieve delicious results nonetheless. I like to serve them with shepherd's salad (page 112) and a bowl of garlic yoghurt or cacık (page 62) for dunking the crusts. For a little more heat add finely chopped fresh red chilli, or scatter with chilli flakes to serve. This is plenty for 4 hungry people but could serve more.

MAKES 4

For the dough:
1 tablespoon active dried yeast
350 ml (12 fl oz/1⅓ cups) lukewarm water
1 tablespoon sugar
2 tablespoons olive oil
500 g (1 lb 2 oz/4 cups) strong white bread flour
2 teaspoons salt
polenta, cornmeal or semolina (cream of wheat) for dusting

For the topping:
¼ teaspoon cumin seeds
¼ teaspoon coriander seeds
450 g (1 lb/2 cups) minced (ground) lamb
2 tablespoons olive oil
1 tablespoon Turkish red pepper paste (page 214) or 1 teaspoon hot or
    sweet paprika
1 tablespoon Turkish tomato paste or 2 tablespoons concentrated
    tomato purée (paste)
4 tablespoons finely chopped flat-leaf parsley, plus extra to serve
1 teaspoon sumac (optional)
½ onion, very finely chopped
1 large fresh tomato, skinned, deseeded and very finely chopped
1 garlic clove, finely chopped
salt and freshly ground black pepper
lemon wedges to serve

Preheat the oven to its highest setting. Place two baking trays or pizza stones into the oven. Unless you have a big oven, you may need to cook the lahmacun one or two at a time.

Mix the yeast, water, sugar and oil together in a jug. Leave in a warm place for 10–15 minutes to activate the yeast. It should form a thick, frothy head. Thoroughly mix the flour and salt with the yeast liquid in a large mixing bowl. The dough will be fairly sticky at this stage.

On a floured surface, start to knead the dough, using floured hands and knuckles to stretch the dough out, before folding it back on itself. (If it is really too sticky to do this, add a tablespoon or two of flour to the mix.) Knead for 10 minutes, until smooth and elastic.

Place the dough in an oiled bowl, cover with a damp cloth or oiled cling-film (plastic wrap) and leave in a warm place for about an hour or until doubled in size. (Depending on the temperature, it may take longer to double in size. You can tell when it has finished rising as the dough will dent rather than spring back when you press it.)

Meanwhile, make the topping. Toast the cumin and coriander seeds in a dry frying pan for a couple of minutes until fragrant. Remove from the heat and grind lightly in a pestle and mortar. Put the spices and all the other ingredients in a large bowl and mix together using your hands: the end result should be a fairly smooth paste.

Knock back the dough and divide into quarters. On a floured surface and with a floured rolling pin, roll each one into a circle roughly 30 cm (12 in) diameter. Take the hot trays or stones out of the oven, dust them with polenta, cornmeal or semolina, and carefully slide two of the dough circles onto them. Working quickly, smear each dough with a portion of the top-ping, using the back of a spoon to smooth the paste evenly, leaving a border around the edge for the crust.

Cook for 8–10 minutes or until the dough has browned and bubbled slightly. Squeeze over a little fresh lemon juice, sprinkle with some parsley and serve immediately. Repeat with the remaining ingredients.

Photograph overleaf

Kabaklı Lahmacun

Courgette Lahmacun

Lahmacun are traditionally made with meat, but if you'd prefer a vegetarian version, try these. You don't have to use feta: hard or soft goat's cheese, mozzarella or halloumi are all tasty alternatives. You can also experiment with roasted peppers or aubergine.

MAKES 4

For the dough:
1 tablespoon active dried yeast
350 ml (12 fl oz/1½ cups) lukewarm water
1 tablespoon sugar
2 tablespoons olive oil
500 g (1 lb 2 oz/4 cups) strong white bread flour
2 teaspoons salt
polenta, cornmeal or semolina (cream of wheat) for dusting

For the topping:
2 courgettes (zucchini)
2 tablespoons pul biber or mild chilli flakes (or to taste)
4 tablespoons olive oil
4 spring onions (scallions), finely sliced
300 g (10½ oz/2 cups) crumbled feta
freshly ground black pepper

Preheat the oven to its highest setting. Place two baking sheets or pizza stones in the oven. Unless you have a big oven, you may need to cook the lahmacun one or two at a time.

Mix the yeast, water, sugar and oil together in a jug. Leave in a warm place for 10–15 minutes to activate the yeast. It should form a thick, frothy head.

Thoroughly mix the flour and salt with the yeast liquid in a large mixing bowl. The dough will be fairly sticky at this stage. On a floured surface, start to knead the dough, using floured hands and knuckles to stretch the dough out, before folding it back on itself. (If it is really too sticky to do this, add a tablespoon or two of flour to the mix.) Knead for 10 minutes, until smooth

and elastic. Place the dough in an oiled bowl, cover with a damp cloth or oiled clingfilm (plastic wrap) and leave in a warm place for about an hour.

Meanwhile, make the topping: using a potato peeler or mandolin shave the courgettes (zucchini) from top to bottom into thin slices. Toss with the other ingredients and divide into four portions.

Knock back the dough and divide into quarters. On a floured surface and with a floured rolling pin, roll each one into a circle roughly 30 cm (12 in) diameter. Working quickly, take the hot trays or stones out of the oven, dust with polenta, cornmeal or semolina and carefully slide two of the dough circles onto them. Scatter each one with a quarter of the topping, leaving a border around the edge for the crust.

Cook for 8–10 minutes or until the dough has browned and bubbled slightly. Repeat with the remaining ingredients. Serve immediately.

Sigara Böreği

Cigar Borek

I have a deep love for borek, the flaky, stuffed savoury pastries you find all over Istanbul and across the surrounding regions. I had these tube-shaped borek, filled with hot, sharp cheese, as part of a meze one night, and just had to get the recipe.

COOK'S TIP:
In rural Turkey, many women still make *yufka* dough at home, rolling huge circles of paper-thin pastry using a narrow wooden pin called an *oklava*, while in Istanbul you can buy fresh yufka dough on every shopping street from a *yufkaci*. While it is possible to buy yufka outside Turkey, it is easier to find filo (phyllo) which works just as well. If you have a Turkish store nearby, buy circular or triangular sheets of yufka dough. All types dry out very quickly once exposed to air, so once you've opened the packet, cover the sheets with a slightly damp cloth. Because Cigar Borek are deep fried, it's best not to mist the dough with water (as you might to keep filo soft) as it will create blisters on the surface of the dough as it cooks, as well as making the oil spit. For the same reason I don't recommend using frozen dough.

MAKES ABOUT 12
250 g (9 oz) feta
2 tablespoons finely chopped flat-leaf parsley
1 spring onion (scallion), split lengthways and very finely chopped
1 egg, beaten
14–16 sheets of filo (phyllo), or yufka, pastry (see tip above)
vegetable oil for deep-frying

Mash the feta with the parsley and spring onion and mix in the egg. Have ready a bowl of water and a large, dry, non-stick baking tray.

Lay two sheets of filo on top of each other on a clean work surface in front of you, with one of the short sides closest to you. Run a sharp knife through the filo from the far left-hand corner to the bottom right-hand corner nearest you, giving you four triangular sheets of dough, still stacked in twos on top of each other.

Quickly spread a tablespoon of the filling in a line across the shortest side of the right hand of the two piles, the side furthest from you. Leave about 2.5 cm (1 in) of pastry without filling at either end of the line. Tucking the sides of the dough in gently over the filling as you go, to prevent leaks, roll the dough towards you, around the filling and into a tube shape. Don't roll too tightly or the borek may burst. Because the triangles are not even lengths on both sides, tuck a little more dough in on the right-hand side, otherwise there will be more dough wrapped around one end than the other. The aim is to get the bottom point of the triangle of dough to finish roughly in the middle of the tube-shaped borek – like a stretched out croissant (trimming the pastry point into shape before sealing helps).

Dampen the pointed end of pastry with a little water and seal it to the tube. Carefully place each borek on the baking tray while you make the rest. Don't let them touch each other as they will stick together.

Heat a large deep pan of oil until a cube of day-old bread sizzles and browns in 30 seconds. Using a fish slice or wide slotted spoon, gently slide 2 or 3 borek into the hot oil and deep fry for 2–3 minutes, until golden brown. Lift out carefully and drain on paper towel while cooking the rest. Serve as a snack, starter, hot meze dish or with a salad as a light supper.

Although deep-frying these borek is best, they can also be baked. Before starting to roll the borek, preheat the oven to 180°C (350°F/gas 4). Brush with butter first. Place on a buttered baking tray and brush very generously with at least 60g (2 oz/½ stick) melted butter. Bake for 15–20 minutes or until the borek are golden brown and crisp.

Etli Börek

Beef Borek

These little triangles are sometimes grilled (broiled), but I like them baked and buttery. Use this recipe as a basis and experiment.

MAKES 12–14
250 g (9 oz/generous cup) minced (ground) beef
½ onion, finely chopped
1 garlic clove, finely chopped
115 g (4 oz/1 stick) butter
pinch of ground cinnamon
¼ teaspoon ground cumin
1 tablespoon pul biber or 1 teaspoon mild chilli flakes (or to taste)
salt and freshly ground black pepper
2 tablespoons finely chopped flat-leaf parsley
7 or 8 sheets filo (phyllo), or yufka, pastry (see tip, previous page)

In a tiny splash of oil, brown the meat over a medium heat, stirring until all the grains are separate. In a separate pan, soften the onion and garlic in 15 g (½ oz/1 tablespoon) of the butter for 5 minutes. Add the cinnamon, cumin and pul biber or mild chilli flakes, plus salt and pepper. Add the beef to the onion mixture and cook together for five minutes. Taste and adjust the seasonings (you can add more of the spices too, if you like).

Stir in the chopped parsley and 100 ml (3½ fl oz/scant ½ cup) water. Simmer for 8–10 minutes and remove from the heat. Cool. Meanwhile, melt the remaining butter and use a little to grease a large baking sheet. Preheat the oven to 200°C (400°F/gas 6).

Remove the filo or yufka from its packet. Take one sheet from the pile and cover the rest with a slightly damp cloth – it dries out very quickly. Lay the sheet out so one of the longest sides is facing you and cut it in half, leaving you with two rectangles. Brush with melted butter, then fold each in half, longest side to longest side, leaving you with two narrow oblongs. Brush with butter again.

Place a heaped tablespoon of the meat mixture just below the top right-hand corner of the pastry on one of the oblongs. Bring the top left corner of the pastry down, diagonally over the meat, to touch the right-hand side of the pastry, forming a triangle over the filling. Do the same again from the top right-hand corner, this time picking up the meat in its pocket of pastry too. Brush with butter again. Continue to fold like this, zig-zagging all the way down the pastry oblong, folding diagonally across until you

BREADS AND SAVOURY PASTRIES

reach the end of the pastry. You need to fold at least 4 times to seal the
filling in completely. Brush the last flap with butter to seal (trim off any
overhanging pastry if it is too short to fold again).

Place on the baking sheet while you finish the rest of the borek. Bake for
20 minutes, or until golden brown all over. Serve hot as part of a meze or as
a starter.

Pide Ekmeği or Ramazan Pidesi

Turkish Bread

This bread is often eaten during Ramadan, but is eaten during the rest of the year as well. In the UK, we think of this particular loaf as Turkish bread, despite there being dozens of different types baked there. Try thinly slicing, then toasting it and using it to scoop up dips and meze dishes.

MAKES 2 LOAVES
1 tablespoon active dried yeast
350 ml (12 fl oz/1⅓ cups) lukewarm water
1 tablespoon caster (superfine) sugar
2 tablespoons olive oil
500 g (1 lb 2 oz/4 cups) strong white bread flour
1½ teaspoons salt
1 egg yolk
50 ml (2 fl oz/¼ cup) milk
1 teaspoon nigella (black onion) seeds
1 teaspoon sesame seeds
2 tablespoons polenta, cornmeal or semolina (cream of wheat)

Mix the yeast, water, sugar and oil together in a jug. Leave in a warm place for 10–15 minutes to activate the yeast. It should form a thick, frothy head.

In a large bowl, mix together the flour and salt. Gradually add the liquid to the dry ingredients, using your hands to mix it into a thick dough. Using your hands, knead the dough for 10 minutes. The dough will become stretchy, slightly glossy and pliable. Knead until any lumps disappear and the dough is smooth.

Place the dough in a clean oiled bowl and cover with a damp cloth or with oiled clingfilm (plastic wrap). Put the bowl in a warm place for an hour, to allow the dough to rise. (Depending on the temperature, it may take longer to double in size. You can tell when it has finished rising as the dough will dent rather than spring back when you press it.)

Place it on a floured work surface. It will be quite sticky with a soft, stringy honeycomb texture inside, so flour your hands too. Knock back the dough by pressing out the air with your knuckles, and then divide it into two balls. Re-cover the balls and leave to rest for 15–20 minutes.

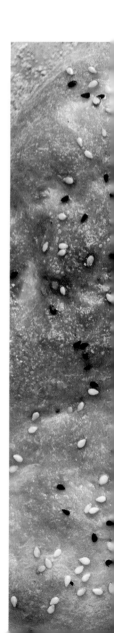

BREADS AND SAVOURY PASTRIES

Meanwhile, preheat the oven to its maximum setting, around 240°C (475°F/gas 9), and place 2 pizza stones or large, upturned baking trays in to heat up.

Whisk together the egg yolk and milk. Flour the work surface and your hands again and firmly flatten each piece of dough into an oblong about 30 × 15 cm (12 × 6 in) and about 1 cm (½ in) thick (if you don't flatten it properly it will rise unevenly).

Remove the hot stones or trays from the oven and dust each with a table-spoon of polenta, cornmeal or semolina. Transfer one of the circles of dough to each stone. (If you like, prepare the dough on a sheet of baking paper, dusted with polenta or semolina as before, and directly transfer the bread on the paper to the stone.) Working quickly, dent the tops of the dough all over with your fingertips, then brush with the egg and milk glaze. Scatter with half the seeds over each, and bake the bread for 10 minutes or until risen and golden all over. Remove from the oven, transfer to a wire rack to cool and eat while still warm.

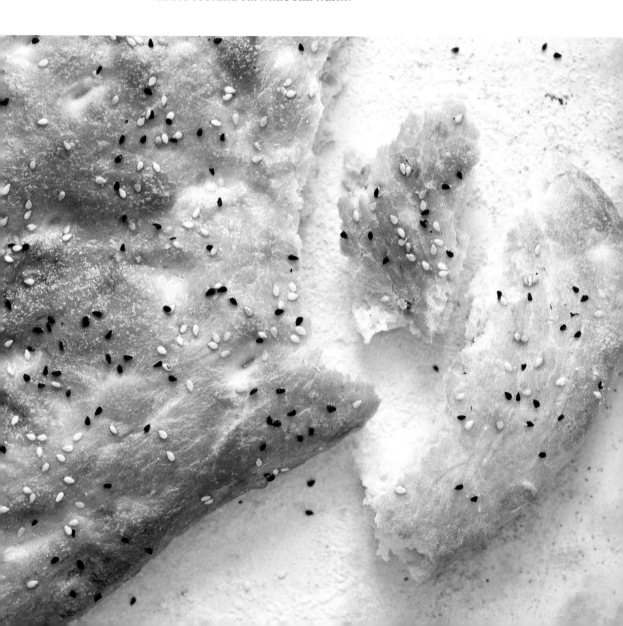

MEZE VE SALATALAR

Mezes and Salads

Mezes are for special occasions, and are meant to be shared and eaten slowly. Many restaurants don't have menus, but will bring round huge trays of meze for you to pick from – perhaps mackerel with a piquant mustard sauce, crisp fried anchovies, crunchy fennel with pomegranate seeds or garlicky dips made with courgette, aubergine (eggplant) or broad beans.

Cacık

Yoghurt Dip

Cacık is a garlicky yoghurt sauce that is often served alongside grilled meats as well as as a meze dish. Its close cousin is *haydari,* often served alongside raki, an aniseed spirit, and made with very thick strained yoghurt called *süzme.* (To make süzme, line a colander with clean muslin or a clean dish cloth and drain three times the quantity of yoghurt in it over a sink or bowl overnight and continue as for the recipe below). Cacık is sometimes diluted with water or milk to make it soupier.

SERVES 4
2 teaspoons finely chopped dill
250 ml (8½ fl oz/1 cup) plain Turkish or Greek-style yoghurt
60 g (2 oz/⅓ cup) grated cucumber, liquid squeezed out
1 garlic clove, finely chopped and mashed to a paste
1 tablespoon olive oil
½ teaspoon dried mint (optional)
1 teaspoon freshly squeezed lemon juice (or to taste)
salt

Mix 1 teaspoon of the dill with the yoghurt, cucumber, garlic and olive oil. Taste and add the mint, if using, lemon juice and salt gradually, tasting until you have a tangy sauce, flavoured to your liking. Spoon into a small serving bowl and garnish with the remaining teaspoon of chopped dill.

Didem's Mücver

Courgette Fritters

Chef Didem Senol is famous for her *mücver* and so many people asked for the recipe that she wrote it on a mirror in her restaurant, Lokanta Maya. I often serve these alongside a bowl of cacık (page 62).

SERVES 4–8
450 g (1 lb) courgettes (zucchini), coarsely grated
salt and freshly ground black pepper
2 large or 3 small spring onions (scallions), finely chopped
100 g (3½ oz/⅔ cup) crumbled feta
1 tablespoon finely chopped flat-leaf parsley
2 tablespoons finely chopped dill
100 g (3½ oz/generous ¾ cup) plain (all-purpose) flour
½ teaspoon baking powder
2 eggs, beaten
vegetable oil for deep frying

Sprinkle the grated courgettes lightly with salt in a colander. Toss them gently then leave to drain over a sink or bowl for 10 minutes. Rinse with cold water and drain thoroughly.

Mix the courgette with the onions, feta and herbs. Taste to check the seasoning, then add the flour, baking powder and eggs. Mix together thoroughly: it will be a fairly wet dough, but should be firm enough to hold together if you pick up a spoonful and let it slide off back into the bowl. Add a little more flour if necessary.

Heat oil for deep-frying until shimmering and a cube of day-old bread sizzles and browns in 30 seconds. Turn the heat down to medium. Using a dessert spoon carefully drop scoops of the mixture into the hot oil. Do this in batches. Cook for 1½ minutes until golden brown and cooked through. You should be able to make 15–16 fritters. Remove with a slotted spoon and drain on paper towels.

If you prefer to shallow-fry the fritters, shape the mix into flat patties and cook in about 1 cm (½ in) hot vegetable oil. Allow them to fully brown before flipping them over, otherwise they will fall apart. Serve hot.

Patlıcan Ezmesi

Smoky Aubergine Dip

This dip is made with aubergines (eggplants) cooked by charring them whole and with the skin on, over a gas ring, on a barbecue or under the grill (broiler). It's another dish which comes in all sorts of different guises in Istanbul – you can add anything from grilled (bell) peppers to a dollop of plain yoghurt or roasted tomatoes to transform it into something quite different, but equally moreish. The crucial thing, though, is that you burn the aubergines thoroughly. A great Istanbul chef, Gencay Ucok, who runs a restaurant called Meze by Lemon Tree, gave me this advice: "If you think the aubergines are done, they're not done. And if you run them under water to remove the skins, you'll wash out all the flavour." And he is quite right.

SERVES 4
3 large aubergines (eggplants)
3 tablespoons lemon juice
2 garlic cloves, crushed
3 tablespoons olive oil
1 tablespoon finely chopped flat-leaf parsley
salt

To char the aubergines, if using a gas hob, place a sheet of foil around the bottom of the ring, below the gas, to protect the hob from drips. If using a grill (broiler), turn it up to its highest setting. Place the aubergines as close to the heat as possible (directly onto the ring if using gas) and allow each side to scorch until the skin is blackened and blistering and the flesh is beginning to collapse. Turn to ensure even cooking. This will take 30 minutes under the grill, or around 15–20 minutes per aubergine on a gas ring, depending on size.

Place the charred vegetables in a bowl and splash 1 tablespoon of the lemon juice over each one. Allow to cool. Lay them on a board and split lengthways down the middle. Scoop out the flesh, avoiding the black, charred skin as much as possible. Some Turkish cooks avoid any flesh that is slightly discoloured, but I like the intense smoky flavour it gives to this dish. (If you want to avoid discoloured flesh, you will need to blacken another aubergine to get enough untainted flesh.)

Squeeze the flesh to remove excess moisture – it will be quite wet – and transfer to a serving bowl. Add the garlic, olive oil, parsley and a little salt, to taste. Mash it gently with a fork – not too much or you will lose its pleasing, chunky texture. Serve as part of a meze with flatbreads or crudités.

Hıyar Salatası

Cucumber and Walnut Salad

The crunchy, slightly bitter walnuts blend beautifully with the sweet-sharp pomegranate seeds and cooling cucumber in this very refreshing salad. It's a lovely meze dish but also goes particularly well with grilled halloumi, or any fish or poultry.

SERVES 4
400 g (14 oz) cucumber
1 teaspoon pul biber or mild chilli flakes
1 teaspoon salt
150 g (5 oz/1¼ cups) roughly chopped walnuts
seeds of ½ pomegranate
4 tablespoons olive oil
2 tablespoons lemon juice
1 garlic clove, crushed, or to taste

Split the cucumber in half, and using a teaspoon, scoop out the seeds and discard. Slice the flesh into semicircles and mix together with the pul biber or mild chilli flakes, salt, walnuts and pomegranate seeds in a serving dish. Whisk together the olive oil and lemon juice then add the garlic. Pour this dressing over the salad and toss to combine.

Havuç Mücveri

Carrot Fritters

I first had carrot fritters at Dai Pera, a pretty little restaurant in Beyoğlu specialising in *ev yemekleri* or Turkish home-style cooking. It is run by one of Istanbul's growing band of female restaurateurs, the lovely Arzu Gürdamar.

SERVES 4–8
1 teaspoon cumin seeds
½ teaspoon coriander seeds
250 g (9 oz/1⅔ cups) coarsely grated carrot
2 large or 3 small spring onions (scallions), finely chopped
2 tablespoons finely chopped dill
1 tablespoon finely chopped flat-leaf parsley
finely grated zest of ½ lemon
100 g (3½ oz/⅔ cup) crumbled feta
salt and freshly ground black pepper
100 g (3½ oz/generous ¾ cup) plain (all-purpose) flour
½ teaspoon baking powder
3 eggs, beaten
vegetable oil for deep frying

In a dry pan, toast the cumin and coriander seeds until they just release their scent. Take off the heat straight away and grind to a powder with a pestle and mortar.

Mix the carrot and spring onion with the dill, parsley, lemon zest, ground spices and feta. Taste and season as necessary. Then add the flour, baking powder and eggs. Mix thoroughly. The mixture should be firm enough to stick together. Add a tablespoon of flour if it's too wet.

Heat the oil for deep-frying until shimmering and a cube of day-old bread sizzles and browns in 30 seconds. Turn the heat down to medium. Using a dessert spoon, scoop the mixture into rough patties and slide into the hot oil, carefully, in batches (you should make 15–16 fritters). Cook for 2 minutes if you like a soft centre, or 3 minutes for an extra-crisp shell and firm centre. Remove with a slotted spoon and drain on paper towel. Serve hot.

If you prefer to shallow-fry the fritters, shape the mix into flat patties and cook in about 1 cm (½ in) of hot vegetable oil. Allow them to fully brown before flipping them over, otherwise they will fall apart.

Sürk Salatası

Sürk Salad

Sürk is a spicy cheese made around Antakya in southern Turkey. I had this salad, in which the cheese is crumbled and whisked into a dressing, in a little restaurant called Babel in Cihangir, which specialises in food from Antakya. Because sürk is very hard to find in the UK, I use feta and add a little fresh chopped chilli. If you're lucky enough to find some sürk, omit the chilli.

SERVES 4
½ cucumber
1 spring onion (scallion), finely sliced
2 large, ripe tomatoes, cut in to bite-sized pieces
1 fresh red chilli (or to taste), deseeded and finely chopped
1 large bunch of parsley
60 g (2 oz) feta
3–4 tablespoons olive oil

Chop the cucumber into quarters, lengthways, then into 5 mm (¼ in) slices and place in a salad bowl. Add the spring onion, tomatoes and chilli. Remove the parsley leaves from the stalks, discard the stalks (use to flavour stock or soup) and roughly chop the leaves. Add to the bowl.

Using your fingers, crumble the feta as finely as possible. Add 3 tablespoons of the olive oil to the cheese and whisk together with a fork. Pour about half of the dressing over the salad and toss to combine. Add more dressing to taste, adding the extra oil if necessary: the salad should not be too oily. Serve immediately.

Kabak Salatası

Pumpkin Dip

This is an unusual dish because, in Turkey, pumpkin is almost never used in savoury dishes. I discovered this in an excellent kebab house, Zubeyir, near İstiklal Caddesi, the busiest shopping street in Istanbul.

SERVES 4
500 g (1 lb 2 oz) pumpkin or squash
vegetable oil for cooking
4 heaped tablespoons plain Turkish or Greek-style yoghurt
1 garlic clove, crushed
1 teaspoon lemon juice
1 tablespoon olive oil
1 small fresh red chilli, deseeded and finely chopped (optional)
salt and freshly ground black pepper
pul biber or mild chilli flakes to serve

Preheat the oven to 180°C (350°F/gas 4). Peel and deseed the pumpkin or squash, then chop into 2.5 cm (1 in) chunks. Toss in a little vegetable oil and roast for 35 minutes but don't allow to brown too much – cover with foil if necessary.

Remove the squash from the oven and tip into a bowl, leave to cool, then mash and chill until ready to serve. Season to taste and sprinkle with pul biber or mild chilli flakes.

Ispanak Nar Salatası

Spinach and Pomegranate Salad

This lovely salad, speckled with ruby-red pomegranate seeds among the green spinach and golden pine nuts, complements chicken, meat or fish perfectly. It also makes a delicious starter or meze dish.

SERVES 4
250 g (9 oz) fresh spinach
4 tablespoons pine nuts (pine kernels)
seeds from ½ pomegranate

For the dressing:
1 tablespoon lemon juice
1 tablespoon olive oil
salt and freshly ground black pepper

Wash the spinach thoroughly and remove any thick pieces of stalk. Pat dry with paper towels and place in a serving bowl. Gently toast the pine nuts in a dry pan until golden (watch carefully as they burn easily).

Tip the pine nuts into the bowl with the spinach and add the pomegranate seeds. Whisk the lemon juice and oil together with a little salt and pepper to taste. Drizzle over the salad. Toss together and serve.

*Piles of pomegranates sit outside
Istanbul's grocery stores, some with
their tops trimmed away, to show
off the juicy red seeds within.*

Havuç Salatası

Carrot Salad

This is like a much zestier and more flavoursome version of coleslaw, the sharpness of yoghurt and lemon being a great foil for the sweet richness of carrot and nutty tahini. Tahini is a paste made from sesame seeds and you can find it in supermarkets and Middle Eastern stores. You can also cook the grated carrot until slightly caramelised before cooking and dressing. If so, you'll need another 100g of carrots.

SERVES 4
120ml (4 fl oz/½ cup) plain Turkish or Greek-style yoghurt
1 garlic clove, crushed
2 teaspoons tahini (sesame paste)
1 tablespoon lemon juice
salt to taste
200 g (7 oz/1⅓ cups) coarsely grated carrot

Whisk the yoghurt, garlic, tahini and lemon juice together in a salad bowl until thoroughly blended. Season to taste. Gently stir in the grated carrot. Taste and re-season if necessary. Leave to stand for 30 minutes before serving, if you have time, to allow the flavours to develop.

Patlıcan Salatası

Aubergine and Sweet Pepper Salad

Here, the aubergines are simmered with tomatoes then mixed with roasted red pepper to created a cooked vegetable dish that is always referred to as a salad.

SERVES 4
2–3 aubergines (eggplants), about 600g (1 lb 5 oz) total weight
lemon juice
½ teaspoon salt
1 red (bell) pepper
75 ml (2½ fl oz) olive oil
1 tablespoon Turkish tomato paste or concentrated tomato purée (paste)
3 juicy tomatoes, cored, deseeded and sliced into small chunks
1 garlic clove, very finely sliced

Preheat the oven to 180°C (350°F/gas 4). Chop the aubergines into 2 cm (¾ in) cubes. Squeeze over a little lemon juice and toss them in the salt. Place in a colander over a sink or bowl for 10 minutes to drain.

Cut the pepper in half and discard the seeds and any membrane from the inside. Roast in the oven, cut sides down, on a baking tray for 25 minutes. When ready they will be lightly brown and beginning to collapse. Place in a plastic bag or plastic box with lid and allow to cool. This will make it easier to peel off the skin. Remove skin and discard, then slice the flesh into strips.

Meanwhile, put 3 tablespoons of the oil in a large heavy-based pan over a low heat. Add the aubergines and cook very slowly, until thoroughly soft and tender, and lightly browned. This may take 45 minutes to 1 hour, stirring and turning as necessary.

Add the tomato paste to the aubergines and cook for 2 minutes. Then add the fresh tomatoes and roasted pepper slices plus a further 2 tablespoons of the olive oil. Cook for 2–3 minutes over a low heat, until the tomatoes are just starting to fall apart but still retaining their shape. Remove from the heat and stir in the garlic slivers. Serve when just warm or cold.

Patlıcan Kızartması

Crispy Aubergines

With the simple tomato sauce and garlic yoghurt, these make a great warm meze dish, or quick vegetarian supper.

SERVES 2–4
1 large aubergine (eggplant)
¼ teaspoon salt
vegetable oil for deep-frying
bread and a green salad to serve

For the tomato sauce:
250 ml (8 ½ fl oz/1 cup) passata (sieved puréed tomatoes)
2 tablespoons olive oil
1 garlic clove, roughly crushed but still whole

For the garlic yoghurt:
1 garlic clove, crushed
200 ml (7 fl oz/generous ¾ cup) plain Turkish or Greek-style yoghurt
pinch of salt

Using a sharp knife, slice the aubergine into rounds about 5 mm (¼ in) thick. Sprinkle with the salt and toss. Put the slices in a colander over a sink or bowl to drain for 10 minutes.

Bring the tomato sauce ingredients to the boil in a saucepan over a medium heat. Season and simmer for 15 minutes until thickened, stirring occasionally. Remove the garlic. Mix the garlic yoghurt ingredients together.

Meanwhile, heat about 5 cm (2 in) vegetable oil in a deep saucepan until shimmering and a cube of day-old bread browns in 30 seconds. Dry the aubergine slices slightly on both sides with paper towel. Deep-fry in batches, for about 3 minutes until golden brown on both sides, turning once. They should still be soft and creamy inside.

Drain the cooked slices on paper towel and keep warm. When all the aubergine slices are golden and crispy, lay them out flat on two warm plates. Drizzle over the tomato sauce and place a dollop of garlic yoghurt in the middle. Serve with bread, for mopping up juices, and a fresh green salad.

Pancar Ezmesi

Beetroot Dip

The beetroot (red beets) are roasted in their skins to retain all their sweet earthiness (they are also much easier to peel once cooked). Trim off any leaves and stems but leave the root intact – just wash well to remove any dirt or grit before you cook them.

SERVES 4
200 g (7 oz) raw beetroot (beets), left whole and unpeeled
1 tablespoon olive oil, plus 1 teaspoon per beetroot, for roasting
3 tablespoons plain Turkish or Greek-style yoghurt
1 garlic clove, crushed
salt

Preheat the oven to 180°C (350°F/gas 4). Rub each beetroot with 1 teaspoon of oil and sprinkle with a little salt. Wrap the beetroots in foil and roast for an hour at until they are soft and offer no resistance to the point of a knife. Remove from the oven.

When cool enough to handle, strip off the tough outer skin: use your thumbs to rub it off. Quarter and place in a blender with the olive oil, yoghurt and garlic, and blitz until smooth. Taste and adjust the seasoning if necessary. Serve with slices of warm flat bread or raw vegetables, for dipping and scooping.

Közlenmiş Kırmızı Biber

Smoky Red Peppers with Garlic

These formed part of a long lazy lunch one hot June afternoon in Istanbul, watching kittens chase each other across the restaurant's terrace.

COOK'S TIP:
You can roast or grill (broil) the peppers for this dish, but the smokiest flavour comes from charring them directly over a gas ring.

SERVES 2-4
3 red (bell) peppers
1 garlic clove
200 ml (7 fl oz/generous ¾ cup) olive oil or enough to cover

Line the area around the gas ring with foil. Turn on the flame and put the peppers directly over the heat. When the bottom of each pepper begins to blacken and blister, turn, using tongs. Once the peppers have charred, remove from the gas ring. Place in a plastic bag or plastic box with a lid and leave to cool – this makes them easier to peel.

Once cool, gently rub and peel off the skins. (If possible, resist the urge to rinse them as this will wash off some of the flavour.) Cut the peppers in half and remove the seeds and stalks. Cut into 2.5 cm (1 in) thick strips and place in a small serving bowl.

Slice the garlic as finely as possible and add to the bowl. Cover with olive oil and stand until ready to serve – the longer they're left, the more garlicky they'll be. Serve at room temperature.

Kabak Ezmesi

Creamy Courgette and Walnut Dip

If you like, you can use ground almonds instead of walnuts in this fresh and tasty dip.

SERVES 4

1 large courgette (zucchini), coarsely grated
½ tablespoon olive oil
150 ml (5 fl oz/⅔ cup) plain Turkish or Greek-style yoghurt, at room
    temperature
½ garlic clove, crushed
1 spring onion (scallion), split in half lengthways and very finely
    chopped
20 g (¾ oz/¼ cup) walnut pieces
salt to taste

Squeeze out the liquid from the grated courgette. Heat the oil in a frying pan and sauté it very gently with little salt for about 12 minutes, until soft but not brown. When all the moisture has evaporated, set aside to cool.

When cool, mix the courgette with the yoghurt, garlic and spring onion. Roughly crush the walnuts in a pestle and mortar, leaving some pieces larger for texture, and add them to the mix. Taste and adjust the seasoning as necessary.

Arpa Salatası

Spicy Barley Salad

Barley has a lovely nutty taste and a firm texture that makes this a filling salad. You could also try it with coarse burghul (bulgur) or even couscous instead of barley. Use the same amount of balsamic vinegar if you can't get pomegranate molasses.

SERVES 4
100 g (3½ oz/½ cup) pearl barley
1 large bunch of flat-leaf parsley, roughly chopped
1 fresh red chilli, deseeded and finely chopped
seeds of ½ pomegranate
30 g (1 oz/generous ¼ cup) walnut pieces, chopped to the same size
   as the pomegranate seeds

For the dressing:
2 tablespoons olive oil
1 tablespoon pomegranate molasses
salt and freshly ground black pepper

Cook the barley in plenty of boiling, salted water for 30–40 minutes or until tender but still slightly nutty. Drain, rinse with cold water and drain again then tip into a bowl.

Stir the parsley, chilli, pomegranate seeds and chopped walnuts into the barley. Whisk together the dressing ingredients, taste to check seasoning and sharpness and then drizzle over the salad. Toss gently before serving.

MEZES AND SALADS

There is little better on a hot Istanbul day, than ordering a spread of meze dishes, fresh, crunchy salads and warm breads, then lingering at the table with a cold bottle of wine.

Kereviz Ezmesi

Celeriac Dip

We ate this in a little underground *meyhane* (pub), which looked very simple from the outside, but which served a terrific range of unusual meze.

SERVES 4
150 g (5 oz) celeriac (celery root)
150 ml (5 fl oz/⅔ cup) plain Turkish or Greek-style yoghurt
1 teaspoon finely chopped dill
1 tablespoon olive oil
1 garlic clove, crushed (optional)
1 heaped tablespoon mayonnaise
salt to taste

Peel and coarsely grate the celeriac into a bowl. Quickly mix it with all the rest of the ingredients (if you leave it uncovered it will go brown). Taste to see if salt is needed. Serve at room temperature or chilled.

Tarator

Yoghurt and Walnut Sauce

This is perfect with fish and seafood – particularly calamari (page 151).

SERVES 4
1 tablespoon pine nuts (pine kernels)
20 g (¾ oz/scant ¼ cup) roughly chopped walnuts
75 ml (2½ fl oz/scant ⅓ cup) plain Turkish or Greek-style yoghurt
½ garlic clove
1 tablespoon olive oil
1 teaspoon finely chopped dill
salt to taste

Lightly toast the pine nuts in a dry pan. Remove from the pan immediately. In a pestle and mortar, pound the pine nuts and walnuts until finely ground. Mix with all the other ingredients. Taste and add a little salt if necessary.

Pastırmalı Patates

Sautéed Potatoes with Pastırma

Pastırma is salted and air-dried beef which is flavoured with spices like chilli pepper and fenugreek, as well as garlic. It's similar to pastrami, which is easier to get outside Turkey and could easily be used instead.

SERVES 2–4
3–4 large potatoes, scrubbed
olive oil for frying
2–3 slices of pastırma or pastrami, shredded into thin strips
1 teaspoon finely chopped rosemary leaves
2 tablespoons finely chopped fresh flat-leaf parsley
1 spring onion (scallion), sliced
1 teaspoon lemon juice (or more to taste)
salt and freshly ground black pepper

Chop the potatoes into 2.5 cm (1 in) chunks. Parboil in salted water for 10 minutes and then drain in a colander, allowing them to dry slightly. Heat 2 tablespoons of olive oil in a large frying pan and sauté the potatoes in the hot oil for about 15 minutes, until lightly golden and cooked through.

Add the pastırma, rosemary, parsley and spring onion and sauté for a couple of minutes, until the meat is crispy. Remove from the heat, squeeze over a little lemon juice and season with salt and pepper. Serve warm.

Fava

Broad Bean Dip (with Crispy Herbed Flatbreads)

Fava is traditionally made with dried broad (fava) beans, soaked overnight then boiled until soft, then mixed with roasted onion, oil, salt and sugar before being blended, chilled until set and sliced into firm wedges, often scattered with dill. Although the original is delicious, this cheat's version is considerably quicker and is packed with fresh green flavours.

COOK'S TIP:
The moreish crispy flatbreads can be made to go with any meze dish.

SERVES 4
500 g (1 lb 2 oz/3 cups) frozen broad (fava) beans
½ onion, finely chopped
2 tablespoons olive oil
1 teaspoon finely chopped dill (or more to taste)
salt to taste

For the crispy herbed flatbreads:
4–6 flatbreads, homemade and freshly cooked (page 40),
    or from a packet
60 g (2 oz /½ stick) butter, melted
2 tablespoons finely chopped flat-leaf parsley
pul biber or mild chilli flakes

Blanch the broad beans in a pan of boiling salted water for 2 minutes. Remove from heat and run under cold water to refresh. Pop the beans out of their pods, and discard the pods. Sprinkle the chopped onion with a little salt, and massage it into the flesh with your fingertips. Next, soften the onion in the olive oil over a gentle heat; do not allow it to colour. Add the beans and 100 ml (3½ fl oz/generous ⅓ cup) water and bring to the boil. Remove from the heat and purée in a blender or food processor. Cool, then chill in the fridge.

When you're ready to serve, make the flatbreads: preheat the grill (broiler) to medium. Brush each bread with a little melted butter on both sides and place under the grill. Allow to brown and become slightly crispy, a matter of 1–2 minutes. Remove from the grill and scatter with parsley and chilli flakes. Slice into wedges.

Finally, add the dill to the broad bean dip and taste to check the seasoning before serving with the bread wedges for scooping.

Gâvurdağı Salatası

Tomato, Walnut and Pomegranate Molasses Salad

Nuts feature heavily in Turkish salads and this is no exception. If you don't have pomegranate molasses, use balsamic vinegar in the dressing instead.

SERVES 4

400 g (14 oz/2 cups) variety of tomatoes, chopped and drained
50 g (1¾ oz/generous ⅓ cup) roughly chopped walnuts
3 tablespoons chopped flat-leaf parsley
1 tablespoon olive oil
1 teaspoon pomegranate molasses
salt and freshly ground black pepper
lemon juice or sumac (optional)

Put the tomatoes in a bowl and add the walnuts and parsley. Drizzle with the oil and molasses, season lightly and toss gently. Taste and add more pomegranate molasses or, for a sharper salad, a little lemon juice or a dusting of sumac, if you have some to hand.

Kırmızı Turp ve Rezene Salatası

Fennel with Radishes and Sumac

The crunchy texture and aniseed flavour of fennel goes really well with slightly peppery radishes and the sharpness of the sumac. The pomegranate seeds add a juicy tang, but it's good without them too.

COOK'S TIP:
Always put fennel, celeriac (celery root), artichokes and potatoes in acidulated water (water with lemon juice added) once cut if you aren't using them immediately, or they will discolour quickly.

SERVES 4
3 tablespoons lemon juice
1 small fennel bulb, about 200 g (7 oz)
200 g (7 oz/1½ cups) radishes
3 tablespoons olive oil
seeds of ¼ pomegranate (optional)
1 teaspoon sumac
salt

Have ready a bowl of water with one of the tablespoons of lemon juice in it. Finely slice the fennel using a mandolin and place in the acidulated water until just ready to serve, to prevent it discolouring.

Finely slice the radishes and place in a bowl. Whisk the oil and remaining lemon juice together. Drain the fennel and mix with the radishes. Drizzle over the dressing and toss gently. Strew the salad over a large serving platter and scatter with the pomegranate seeds, if using. Finish with a dusting of sumac and a little salt then serve straight away.

Pastırmalı Humus

Warm Hummus with Pastırma

It's not unusual to be served hummus warm in Istanbul and it really enhances the garlicky, sesame flavours of the dip. If you'd like to make this vegetarian, just omit the meat.

SERVES 4–6

2 × 400 g (14 oz) cans chickpeas (garbanzo beans)
pinch of cumin seeds
2 garlic cloves, crushed
3 tablespoons tahini (sesame paste)
1 tablespoon olive oil
juice of a lemon (or less)
1 teaspoon salt (or less)
2 slices of pastırma or pastrami

Drain and rinse the chickpeas. Place in a pan of water and bring to the boil. Simmer for 2 minutes then remove from the heat and drain again. Toast the cumin seeds for 2 minutes in a dry pan and grind to a powder in a pestle and mortar.

Mix the chickpeas with 120 ml (4 fl oz/½ cup) water and all the other ingredients, except the lemon, salt and pastırma. Blitz in a food processor or blender. Taste and gradually add the lemon and salt until the balance of flavours is to your liking – you may not need all of it as some canned chickpeas can be salty.

Meanwhile, chop the pastırma or pastrami quite finely. Fry the meat in a hot dry pan until crisp – this will only take a minute. Sprinkle the flakes of hot meat over the warm hummus and serve straight away.

*In the countryside around Istanbul,
the simplest vegetables are combined
to make beautiful salads.*

Börülce Salatası

Black-eyed Bean Salad

The peaceful Prince's Islands are 11 miles and less than an hour from Istanbul by ferry, and whenever the frenetic pace and 17 million residents of the city get too much, they are a perfect place to escape to. I spent one sunny October afternoon in the garden of Kalpazankaya, a clifftop restaurant overlooking a small, isolated bay on Burgazada island, eating this and watching swimmers dive off an old stone jetty.

SERVES 4
400 g (14 oz) can black-eyed beans, drained
3 red (bell) peppers, deseeded and roughly chopped
3 spring onions (scallions), diagonally sliced
1 tablespoon lemon juice
1 tablespoon olive oil
salt and freshly ground black pepper

Bring a pan of water to the boil and add the beans. Simmer for 1 minute. Drain and refresh the beans by rinsing under cold water then drain again.

Mix the beans with the peppers and spring onion in a serving bowl. Add the lemon juice, oil and a little seasoning, then toss. Taste and adjust the seasoning if necessary. Serve straight away.

Peynirli İncir

Figs with Feta and Mint

In Turkey figs are often used when they are green, to make delicious preserves. It's very hard to get unripe figs in the UK, unless you have access to your very own tree, so try this salad which uses, plump, sweet, ripe ones.

SERVES 4
4 ripe figs
100 g (3½ oz) feta, crumbled into pieces
16 mint leaves

Quarter the figs. If serving as a starter, put 4 pieces on each plate. Alternatively place all the fig quarters in a shallow serving bowl. Scatter over the cheese and mint leaves. Serve immediately.

Çoban Salatası

Shepherd's Salad

This is a very important dish in Turkish cooking, a fresh crisp salad that is served as part of most meals when the ingredients are in season.

COOK'S TIP:
This dish contains raw onions, which can be off-putting to some, but the trick is to rub a little salt into the onion well before serving, which softens them and sweetens the taste.

SERVES 4
¼ teaspoon salt
1 tablespoon finely chopped onion
1 spring onion (scallion), finely chopped
450 g (1 lb) ripe tomatoes
250 g (9 oz) cucumber
½ green (bell) pepper
1 heaped tablespoon roughly chopped flat-leaf parsley
1 tablespoon olive oil
juice of ¼ lemon
salt and freshly ground black pepper

Sprinkle the salt over the two types of onion in a bowl and rub it in with your hands. Set aside for 10 minutes. Chop the tomatoes, cucumber and pepper into pieces of a similar size and place in a serving bowl. Add the onions and all the other ingredients to the tomatoes and toss together gently. Taste and adjust the seasoning before serving.

Yaprak Sarma

Spiced Burghul Wrapped in Vine Leaves

What we call stuffed vine leaves, *dolma*, in the UK are thought of as wrapped vine leaves, *sarma*, in Turkey. Dolma is only used as a term to describe things which are stuffed in Turkish-like hollowed out courgettes (zucchini) or tomatoes, or even stuffed squid. Whatever you'd like to call them, these vine leaves, filled with bright red, slightly fiery burghul (bulgur) wheat, are delicious. They are also easy to assemble.

COOK'S TIP:
Vine leaves can be very salty, so be sure to rinse and blanch them. You can also make this dish with just-blanched chard leaves.

MAKES ABOUT 30
250 g (9 oz) pack preserved vine leaves
150 g (5 oz/scant 1 cup) burghul (bulgur) wheat
1 onion, finely chopped
olive oil
2 tablespoons Turkish hot red pepper paste (page 214), or 1 very finely
  chopped red (bell) pepper plus chilli flakes to taste
1 teaspoon pomegranate molasses
2 tablespoons finely chopped flat-leaf parsley
plain Turkish or Greek-style yoghurt to serve

Remove the vine leaves from their packet and rinse under cold running water. Bring a large pan of water to the boil. Slide the vine leaves into the water and blanch for 2 minutes. Drain, rinse again in cold water and drain again.

Put the burghul wheat in a bowl. Just cover with boiling water and leave to soak for 10 minutes, until partially softened. Drain, if necessary, and fluff up with a fork.

Meanwhile, soften the onion in 1 tablespoon of olive oil for 5–10 minutes, stirring, over a low heat until translucent. Then add the red pepper paste, or chopped pepper and chilli flakes, to taste. Cook very gently until pulpy; 5 minutes if using the paste, 10 minutes if using fresh peppers. Add the pomegranate molasses, stir and then add the soaked burghul. Cook for 1 minute, then remove from the heat. Add the parsley.

To stuff the leaves, place a whole, intact leaf on a flat surface with the stem end facing towards you. Remove the stem. Place about 1 tablespoon of the burghul mixture in the middle of the leaf, just above where the stem

MEZES AND SALADS

was. Lift the bottom sections of the leaf up and over the filling, then bring the side edges in over it too. Roll the leaf away from you, folding and catching the edges of the leaf neatly into the roll as you go. When you have rolled the whole leaf up, all the edges should be tucked in to the roll and no filling should be visible. Repeat with more leaves and filling (you should be able to make at least 30 and have a few small or damaged leaves left over).

Use any damaged or particularly small leaves to line the base of a large saucepan or flameproof casserole with a lid. Tightly pack the rolls into the pan, each with the loose edge of the leaf underneath, to prevent it unravelling while cooking. When all the rolls are in the pan, weigh them down with a plate (otherwise they will float and unwrap themselves). Then pour in enough boiling water to just cover the rolls.

Bring to the boil, then turn the heat right down, cover and simmer very gently for 30 minutes. When the rolls have cooked and with the plate still in place, carefully drain the water away. Using tongs, remove the rolls from the pan and transfer to a plate to cool. Serve cold as part of a meze, with a little plain yoghurt.

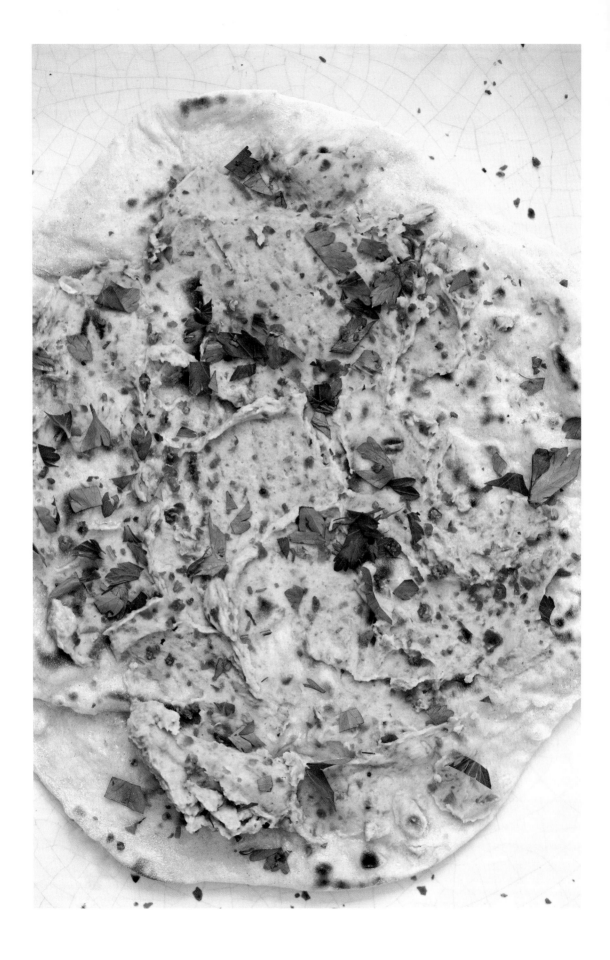

Barbunya Fasulyesi Ezmesi

Borlotti Bean Purée

This recipe was inspired by Didem Senol, the brilliant chef at Lokanta Maya, where she serves shrimp on a lovely nutty borlotti (cranberry) bean purée.

SERVES 4–6
400 g (14 oz) can borlotti (cranberry) beans
1 garlic clove, finely chopped
2 tablespoons olive oil
1 tablespoon lemon juice
salt and freshly ground black pepper
pul biber or mild chilli flakes and chopped flat-leaf parsley to serve

Drain the beans. Place in a pan of water and bring to the boil. Simmer for 2 minutes then remove from the heat and drain.

Place the beans and all the other ingredients in a blender and blitz until a smooth purée is achieved. (For a coarser consistency, mash the beans with a fork.) Taste and adjust the seasoning – you can also add more lemon or garlic, if you like.

Chill before serving, sprinkled with pul biber or mild chilli flakes and some chopped parsley.

ET VE BALİK

Meat and Fish

Although fish and meat are often quite simply cooked in Istanbul, just grilled or fried, there are also lots of delicious and slightly more complex dishes, like the Ottoman chicken stew, *Mahmudiye*, with almonds and dried apricots, *Hünkar Beğendi*, a slow-cooked lamb dish served on top of a smoky creamy aubergine purée, or *Midye Dolma*, mussels stuffed with spiced rice pilaf.

Şiş Kebap

Marinated Lamb Kebabs

Although we associate Turkey with kebabs, many Turkish people argue that they are in fact part of Arab cuisine and a relative newcomer to the city of Istanbul. You can also barbecue these kebabs, just be sure to cook them raised above the heat a little, or the marinade may burn before the meat is cooked. They are hugely popular in Istanbul and are made with every kind of meat available – from chicken to liver.

SERVES 2–4

3 tablespoons hot or mild Turkish red pepper paste (page 214)
1 teaspoon sweet paprika
½ onion, grated
¼ teaspoon freshly ground black pepper
¼ teaspoon salt
2 tablespoons olive oil
500 g (1 lb 2 oz) diced lamb shoulder
warm flatbreads (page 40), shepherd's salad (page 112), garlic yoghurt
    (page 84) or cacık (page 62) to serve

Place all the ingredients except the lamb in a bowl and mix thoroughly. Add the lamb and toss well to ensure every piece gets coated in the marinade. Cover and leave to marinate in the fridge for six hours or overnight.

When ready to cook, thread the meat onto 4 metal skewers. Preheat the grill (broiler) to its highest setting. Grill the kebabs for 3–4 minutes on each side. Serve with warm flatbreads, shepherd's salad and plenty of garlic yoghurt or cacık.

Bıldırcın

Roast Quail

At weekends, the parks and gardens of Istanbul fill with families, meeting to barbecue together, especially where long, narrow strips of grass line the edge of the Bosphorus. Spice-scented smoke wafts over the water late into the evening and these juicy, marinated little birds are a frequently cooked treat. For ease – and because I have fewer chances to barbecue than the residents of sunny Istanbul – I roast them. The skill is to cook them quickly and let them rest before eating to tenderize the flesh.

SERVES 4
4 tablespoons olive oil
1 teaspoon hot or mild Turkish red pepper paste (page 214)
lemon juice
¼ teaspoon thyme leaves
1 lemon cut into 6 wedges
4 garlic cloves, peeled but left whole
8 shallots or baby onions, peeled but left whole
salt and freshly ground black pepper
4 oven-ready quail

Mix everything except the quail together in a large bowl, then coat the quails in the marinade. Leave to marinate for an hour or so. Preheat the oven to 220°C (430°F/gas 8).

Place the marinated quail, lemon wedges, garlic and shallots in an oven tray in a single layer, breast-sides up. Roast for 20–25 minutes, basting the meat once after 15 minutes, or until the birds are golden brown and the skin is crisp. Once they're cooked, let the quail rest in the pan for five or 10 minutes before serving with the juices spooned over. Serve with bread and kısır salad (page 204) or green salad.

Sucuk Dürüm

Sucuk Wrap

These sandwiches, served at make-shift roadside stalls, are a late-night treat much loved by taxi drivers, shift workers, policemen and revellers alike: the rich garlic and beef *sucuk* sausage, with sweet-sharp pickled cabbage, chilli peppers, fresh onion and chunks of tomato is exactly the kind of thing you need to keep going into the night. You can buy pickled cabbage in jars.

I ate my first sucuk wrap at midnight, near Istanbul's outdoor concert stadium, on a plastic seat perched on a kerb, next to some busy traffic lights and with an ice-cold bottle of water. It was exactly what I needed.

COOK'S TIP:
Pickled white cabbage is available at Turkish grocers or you could use well-drained sauerkraut instead.

SERVES 1
1 beef sucuk sausage (you could also use pork sausage, chorizo or other beef sausage)
a few slices of onion
salt
1 flatbread, warmed (see page 40)
1 teaspoon hot or mild red pepper paste, optional (page 214)
1 grilled long green pepper (page 210), deseeded
pickled white cabbage
½ tomato, thickly sliced
roughly chopped flat-leaf parsley

Diagonally slice the sausage into roughly 1 cm (½ in) chunks. Set a frying pan over a medium heat and fry the sausage chunks, turning often, in a tiny splash of olive oil until browned, 3–4 minutes. Sprinkle the onions with a pinch of salt.

To assemble the sandwich, smear a warm flatbread with a little red pepper paste, if using. Scatter the bread with the grilled green pepper, a little white cabbage, the tomato, then the onion, then top with the hot sausage. Scatter over the parsley and wrap: tuck the bottom of the bread in before rolling to keep the filling from falling out. Devour quickly, with plenty of paper napkins to hand.

Adana Kebabi

Adana-style Kebabs

The grill masters – *usta* – of the city of Adana in southern Turkey are famous for cooking the best kebabs. True Adana kebabs are so fiercely protected that they have recently been given a Controlled Designation of Origin by the Turkish patents office. You can easily find delicious Adana-style kebabs in Istanbul too, where they are made to similarly exacting standards: with hand-minced (ground) lamb, lamb's tail fat, sweet red pepper and salt plus, occasionally, garlic and chilli too, moulded into sausage shapes and impaled on long skewers before being cooked over charcoal. (Urfa kebabs are less spicy.)

COOK'S TIP:
Although these kebabs are fine made with leaner minced lamb from a supermarket, they are far better made with rich fatty lamb from a butcher. Somewhat sacrilegiously, I add grated onion to mine. You can also barbecue Adana-style kebabs: cook them raised off the heat and turn more frequently to ensure they cook through without the outside burning. Brush the peppers with oil and barbecue alongside, turning once or twice.

SERVES 4
For the kebabs:
500 g (1 lb 2 oz/2¼ cups) minced (ground) fatty lamb
½ onion, grated
½ teaspoon salt
1 heaped teaspoon hot or mild red pepper paste (page 214), or 1–2 fresh
    red chillies, or ¼ red (bell) pepper, deseeded and very finely chopped
1 tablespoon finely chopped flat-leaf parsley
pinch of pul biber or mild chilli flakes
½ garlic clove, crushed

To finish:
4 flatbreads (page 40)
1 red (bell) pepper, deseeded and cut in to 8 pieces
1 green (bell) pepper, deseeded and cut into 8 pieces
red pepper paste (optional, page 214)
sumac onions (page 216)
finely chopped flat-leaf parsley
garlic yoghurt (page 84)

Mix together all the kebab ingredients and knead them together with your hands. Set aside while you prepare the rest of the ingredients. Preheat the grill (broiler) to maximum. Warm the flatbreads under the grill or in a low oven and keep warm.

Divide the kebab meat into 4 portions. Begin forming the meat around the skewer: take a small handful of the meat and form into an oblong. Slide it along the skewer to the top and squeeze it gently but firmly around the metal to form a sausage shape around the skewer.

Once it has adhered to the skewer, take another handful of meat and wrap it around the skewer so that it joins to the first sausage-shaped ball of meat. Continue to do this until you've used up a quarter of the meat and formed a sausage all the way down the skewer. Repeat with all 4 skewers.

The peppers taste best if they cook with the meat juices dripping down onto them, so place them in the grill pan, underneath the rack, or if easier, use a wide oven tray and rest the skewers across it, balancing on the rim. Grill for 4–5 minutes, or until browned, then turn the skewers over and cook for a further 4–5 minutes until the meat is cooked through. You may need to turn or remove the peppers too if they begin to burn.

To serve, smear a little pepper paste onto a warm flatbread, if using. Slide the kebab off the skewer and place it in the middle of the bread. Scatter over some of the sumac onions, a couple of pieces of grilled pepper and some parsley. Finish with a dollop of garlic yoghurt. Roll up and eat immediately.

Uskumru

Grilled Mackerel with Mustard Mayonnaise

I first tried this one hot and sticky evening in a *meyhane* (pub) in Beyoglu. The fish was served completely covered in sauce, but once we'd scooped out a mouthful or two we realised that the presentation didn't matter at all – the rich oily fish is a perfect match for the thick piquant sauce. It also works well with smoked mackerel, another Turkish favourite.

SERVES 4
4 mackerel fillets
salt and freshly ground black pepper
100 ml (3½ fl oz/scant ½ cup) mayonnaise
2 heaped teaspoons mustard (I like to use half Dijon and half bright
    yellow English mustard)
2 teaspoons white wine vinegar

Preheat the grill (broiler) to its highest setting. Season the fish. Place the fish skin-side down on the grill rack and cook for 4 minutes, then flip and cook the other side, until the skin is browned and blistered. (If you prefer, you can barbecue or pan-fry the mackerel fillets – they will need about 3 minutes each side.) Meanwhile, mix together the mayonnaise, mustards and vinegar. Serve the fish hot with a dollop of the sauce.

Kuzu Pirzola

Marinated Lamb Chops

Juicy lamb chops served with piles of sumac-dusted onions are a staple of Istanbul restaurants.

SERVES 4
For the marinated lamb:
½ onion, grated
3 tablespoons olive oil
juice of ½ lemon
1 garlic clove, roughly chopped
1 teaspoon dried thyme
salt and freshly ground black pepper
4–8 lamb chops, depending on size

1 teaspoon vegetable oil for frying

For the garnish:
1 onion, thinly sliced
pinch of salt
1 teaspoon sumac
2 tablespoons finely chopped flat-leaf parsley

Mix all the marinade ingredients except the lamb together in a large bowl. Add the lamb chops and coat in the marinade. Cover and leave in the fridge overnight.

When ready to cook, heat a frying pan until very hot. Add a teaspoon of vegetable oil. Fry the lamb chops for 2 minutes on each side, or until done to your liking: if you press the meat with your finger and it feels soft, it is rare; if firm, then it is well done. Meanwhile, mix the onion with the sumac, salt and parsley. Serve the hot chops with a little heap of onions.

Etli Köfte

Beef Köfte with Pitta and Tomato Sauce

On one of our Istanbul trips, we stayed in the Marti Hotel, a posh new spot north of buzzing Taksim Square. While devouring a bowl of these meatballs in the hotel restaurant, served with butter-fried chunks of bread, yoghurt and a fresh tomato sauce, we took in the panoramic views of the city. It's tempting to use lean minced (ground) beef, but you need fat to hold them together. Cook shop-bought minced beef all the way through.

SERVES 3–4

For the meatballs:
1 teaspoon coriander seeds
1 teaspoon cumin seeds
500 g (1 lb 2 oz/2¼ cups) minced (ground) beef
¼ teaspoon freshly ground black pepper
pinch of ground cinnamon
½ teaspoon salt
½ onion, grated
2 garlic cloves, crushed
1 teaspoon sweet paprika
vegetable oil for frying

For the tomato sauce:
2 tablespoons olive oil
½ onion, very finely chopped
1 small carrot, very finely diced
1 garlic clove, finely chopped
1 tablespoon Turkish tomato paste or tomato purée (paste)
400 ml (13 fl oz/generous 1¾ cups) passata (sieved puréed tomatoes)

For the pittas:
25 g (scant 1 oz/2 tablespoons) butter
½ pitta bread per person, cut into 2.5 cm (1 in) squares
roughly chopped flat-leaf parsley

For the garlic yoghurt:
200 ml (7 fl oz/generous ¾ cup) plain Turkish or Greek-style yoghurt
1 garlic clove, crushed
salt

For the meatballs, lightly toast the whole spices in a dry pan just until fragrant, about 30 seconds, then grind in a pestle and mortar. Combine all the ingredients (except the oil) together with your hands. Mix only until just blended. Set aside until needed.

For the tomato sauce, heat the oil in a pan and add the onion and carrot. Soften gently, without colouring, for 15 minutes, stirring frequently. Add the garlic and tomato paste. Cook for 3–4 minutes, stirring, then add the passata. Simmer for 10–15 minutes until rich and thick, stirring frequently. Taste to check the seasoning and keep warm until ready to serve.

Meanwhile, finish the meatballs. Heat a large wide frying pan and add 1–2 tablespoons oil. Take a tiny piece of the meatball mix and fry until cooked through. Taste to check the seasoning and adjust if necessary.

Roll the meat mix into 16 small balls. Sauté the meatballs gently in the pan for 5–8 minutes, turning them often, until they are deep brown all over. Break one open to check they are cooked through.

In another pan, melt the butter and when foaming add the pitta bread pieces. Fry the bread until light golden on both sides. Mix the garlic yoghurt together. To serve, scatter a handful of hot pitta pieces in the bottom of each serving bowl. Drizzle with a couple of tablespoons of garlic yoghurt and some tomato sauce. Top with the meatballs and some fresh parsley. Serve straight away.

Ceviche

Ceviche with Lime and Grapefruit

Ceviche is a universal name for raw fish, cured or 'cooked' with citrus, salt and onions. It's not really a traditional Turkish dish, but Turkish chefs are experimenting more and more with techniques from other countries, while still using the wonderful ingredients they can find at home. This dish is a great example – it takes in the Turkish favourite tastes of sour and salt, while using the terrifically fresh fish found in the Black Sea or Sea of Marmara, just a few miles from Istanbul. I was introduced to this dish by the chef Gencay Ucok who serves it at his modern Turkish restaurant, Meze by Lemon Tree in Istanbul.

You need very fresh fish to make ceviche. Buy whole fish with clear eyes and bright red gills from your fishmonger and then get them to fillet it for you. Pre-cut fish from a supermarket isn't suitable for this recipe.

SERVES 4
2 fillets of very fresh sea bass, small bones removed
1 pink grapefruit
1 lime
2 tablespoons capers in brine, rinsed thoroughly
1 tablespoon olive oil
½ teaspoon salt

Slice the fish into thin slices, using your sharpest knife at a 45° angle. Cut the grapefruit in half. Squeeze the juice from one half. Remove the pith and peel from the other half and cut the flesh into thin half moons. Finely slice the lime.

Mix the citrus juices together and add the rinsed capers, olive oil and salt. Lay the fish slices on a plate in a single layer and pour over the citrus juice mix. Lay the slices of grapefruit and lime over the fish. Mix very gently.

Place in the fridge for 30 minutes, then gently turn the fish slices over and check all the fish has come into contact with the salt and citrus juice. Return for a further 30 minutes until the fish is opaque. Transfer to a serving bowl to serve. Eat as a starter or meze.

Balık Ekmek

Fish Sandwich

At night, the watersides of the Golden Horn inlet come alive with people out for supper. While you can spend a lot of money in one of the many fish restaurants, there is little better than a freshly made fish sandwich (almost always mackerel), from one of the dozens of grills that are rolled out every evening. The fish is incredibly fresh, cooked in front of you before being tucked into a baguette alongside thin slivers of salted onion, herbs and juicy tomato. Eating one perched on a wall or plastic stool, with a cold beer in hand, beats most restaurant meals.

SERVES 2
½ onion, halved and thinly sliced into half moons
2 small, long green peppers, or 2 wide strips from a green (bell) pepper
1 baguette
olive oil for brushing
2 mackerel fillets
2 ripe and juicy tomatoes, thickly sliced
red pepper paste (page 214)
pul biber or mild chilli flakes to taste
handful of rocket (arugula)
4 mint sprigs
5–6 dill sprigs
salt and freshly ground black pepper
lemon juice

Sprinkle a little salt over the onions and mix well. Under the grill (broiler) or in a pan over a high heat, cook the peppers or pepper strips, skin-side down, until they begin to char slightly. Remove from the heat.

Cut the baguette into pieces the same length as the fish fillets. Split down the middle and lightly toast both sides, either under the preheated grill or in a griddle pan. Brush the cut sides with olive oil. Keep warm.

Meanwhile, griddle or pan-fry the mackerel fillets over a high heat for 3–4 minutes each side until the skin has begun to crisp up and the fish is cooked through. Take the warm toasted bread and place slices of tomato on one of the cut sides. Smear the other side with a little homemade pepper paste, if using. Place the fish on top of the tomatoes and then add the other ingredients, finishing with grilled pepper and pul biber or mild chilli flakes, if using. Season, squeeze over a little lemon juice, cap with the other half of the bread and eat straightaway.

Hünkar Beğendi

Aubergine Purée Topped with Lamb Stew

This is a rich and satisfying Ottoman dish of lamb stew on a bed of aubergine and cheese, and it smells progressively more delicious as it slowly cooks, making it harder and harder to resist dipping a corner of bread into the pot! The name means the *Sultan's Delight* (or *the Sultan liked it*), and there are two stories about its origins: one is that it was created for a sultan in the 1600s who did indeed like it; the other is that it was served in the nineteenth century Sultan's court to Napoleon's wife, who liked it so much she requested the recipe (the chef refused to give it to her). A salad of bitter leaves with a sharp dressing goes nicely here, or some winter greens.

SERVES 4

For the lamb stew:

850 g (1 lb 14oz) boneless stewing lamb (shoulder, shank or leg), cut into 2.5 cm (1 in) dice, excess fat removed

1 onion, finely chopped

pinch of salt

4 garlic cloves, finely chopped

1 tablespoon Turkish tomato paste or concentrated tomato purée (paste)

2–3 fresh tomatoes, peeled, deseeded and roughly chopped

¼ teaspoon dried thyme

¼ teaspoon dried oregano

200 ml (7 fl oz/generous ¾ cup) hot water

1 tablespoon chopped flat-leaf parsley

For the aubergine purée:

4 large aubergines (eggplants), trimmed

1 tablespoon lemon juice

30 g (1 oz/2 tablespoons) butter

30 g (1 oz/¼ cup) plain (all-purpose) flour

350 ml (12 fl oz/1⅓ cups) milk

60 g (2 oz/½ cup) grated kasseri, parmesan, comté or other hard cheese

salt and freshly ground black pepper

Prepare the lamb. Brown the meat in a deep saucepan with a lid, or a deep flameproof casserole, over a high heat and in batches (if the pan is too crowded the meat will stew rather than caramelise and be less tasty).

Turn the heat down to low, return all the meat to the pan and add the onion and salt. Allow the onion to soften and become translucent for 10 minutes, stirring to prevent sticking, then add the garlic and cook, stirring frequently, for 2 minutes.

Add the tomato paste and cook, stirring again, for a further 2 minutes. Finally add the fresh tomatoes, dried herbs and hot water (the meat should be just covered, so add a little more water if it is not). Stir thoroughly and cover. Simmer for about 2 hours, checking frequently that the sauce is not sticking or reducing too fast – add splashes of hot water whenever necessary to prevent this. The stew is ready when the tomatoes and liquid have reduced and thickened and the meat is just beginning to fall apart.

About 40 minutes before the stew is fully cooked, start the aubergine purée (don't worry if timings over-run – the stew will keep happily with a lid on. You could even make it the day before). Either thoroughly char and blacken their skins for 10 minutes directly over a gas ring (for more details see page 66) or place under a grill (broiler) set to its highest temperature, and allow the skins to blacken and wrinkle, turning them regularly. (If you prefer a less smoky flavour, grill or broil them more slowly, further from the heat.) When the skins are charred, set them aside in a bowl and splash over the lemon juice. Allow them to cool and then scoop out the flesh by splitting each one down the middle with a spoon and using it to gently scrape out the insides. Pull out any large strands of seeds and discard, roughly chop the flesh and place in a colander to drain.

Meanwhile melt the butter in a saucepan big enough to take all the milk and the cooked aubergines, over a low heat. Warm the milk in a separate pan. When the butter is foaming but not brown, add the flour. Mix well and cook over a very low heat for 2 minutes. Slowly add the hot milk, a quarter at a time, stirring to incorporate each time. (Don't add it all at once as the sauce will become lumpy.) When all the milk has been added the sauce should be thick enough to just coat the back of a spoon. If it is too thick, add a little more milk and whisk it in. Add the cheese and the chopped aubergine and cook for 2–3 minutes over the lowest possible heat. Taste and adjust the seasoning with salt and pepper.

Just before serving, stir the parsley into the lamb stew and taste to check the seasoning. Spoon the hot aubergine purée in a thick layer onto a warm serving dish and top with the lamb stew, or serve as individual portions in bowls.

Photograph overleaf

Sumaklı Köfte

Beef Meatballs with Sumac and Garlicky Yoghurt

There are hundreds of different ways of making meatballs, called *köfte*, and even more in the countries surrounding Turkey. There are no hard and fast rules when it comes to making them – they can even be vegetarian – so feel free to play around with the spicing or to try different meats or pulses. Serve these with flatbreads and a shepherd's salad (pages 40 and 112). You can easily make them without sumac, if you can't find it, but it's readily available in Middle Eastern stores and online.

SERVES 2–4

For the meatballs:

3 tablespoons breadcrumbs, plus 1 extra tablespoon if necessary
300 g (10½ oz/generous 1¼ cups) minced (ground) beef
¼ onion, very finely chopped
1 garlic clove, crushed
1 tablespoon very finely chopped flat-leaf parsley
1 teaspoon sumac (optional), plus extra to garnish
1 teaspoon ground cumin
1 teaspoon hot Turkish red pepper paste (page 214) or ½ teaspoon hot paprika
1 teaspoon Turkish tomato paste or 2 teaspoons concentrated tomato purée (paste)
¼ teaspoon freshly ground black pepper
½ teaspoon salt
1 egg, beaten
vegetable oil for deep-frying

For the garlicky yoghurt:

175 ml (6 fl oz/scant ¾ cup) plain Greek-style or Turkish yoghurt
½ garlic clove, crushed (or more)
1 tablespoon finely chopped flat-leaf parsley
salt

If the breadcrumbs are fresh, toast them gently in a dry frying pan. Mix the beef with the onion, garlic, parsley, spices, pastes or purée, seasoning and breadcrumbs. Add the egg and mix quickly but thoroughly. If the mixture is very wet, add the extra breadcrumbs and mix again. Divide the mixture into twelve and shape into balls, using your hands.

To make the garlicky yoghurt sauce, mix the yoghurt with all the other ingredients. Taste and adjust the seasoning. Keep in the fridge until it is time to serve.

Heat the oil for deep-frying until a cube of day-old bread sizzles and browns in 30 seconds, then turn the heat down to low. Deep-fry the meatballs in batches for 4 minutes each, or until the meat in the centre is cooked through and the outside is a deep golden brown (unless you or your butcher freshly grind the meat, it's important to ensure it is thoroughly cooked). Lift out with a slotted spoon and drain on paper towels.

Alternatively flatten into patties and shallow-fry for about 3 minutes on each side until golden and cooked through. Serve straight away, with the yoghurt sauce and sprinkled with a little extra sumac.

Ciğer Tava

Liver with Fresh Onions and Parsley

Istanbullus are obsessed with liver, to the extent that there are dozens of restaurants and street food stalls specialising in it. You can get it deep-fried in batter or grilled in chunks and wrapped up in flatbreads with herbs and tomatoes. You can even buy liver sandwiches from street-corner vendors. This was one of the first liver dishes I tried in Istanbul and remains my favourite.

SERVES 2–4
½ onion, halved and finely sliced into half moons
½ garlic clove, very finely sliced
¼ teaspoon salt and freshly ground black pepper
250 g (9 oz) very fresh lamb's liver
3 tablespoons roughly chopped flat-leaf parsley
1 tablespoon finely chopped dill
pul biber or mild chilli flakes to taste (optional)

Place a large frying pan or griddle pan over a high heat and warm a serving platter. Mix the onion, garlic and salt together in a bowl, to allow them to soften and become sweeter.

Rinse the liver thoroughly and pat it dry with paper towel. Using a very sharp knife, diagonally slice the liver into pieces no more than 1 cm (½ in) thick. Season with salt and pepper and fry quickly for one or two minutes, tossing frequently until browned all over and cooked to your liking (don't overcook or they will become tough).

Place the liver on the warm serving plate and scatter over the onion and garlic mixture, herbs and pul biber or mild chilli flakes, if using. Serve straight away.

Onions, salted to soften and sweeten
them, then scattered with sumac and
pul biber, are a vital part of meals
in Istanbul.

Kalamar

Calamari

To me, a plate of hot, delicate *kalamar* eaten with a bowl of nutty tarator sauce (page 94), looking out over the Bosphorous at sunset, sums up why I love Istanbul's food: it's such a simple dish and really makes the most of local ingredients, plus it's easy to recreate at home. You can use any beer for the batter, but I find dark beers make for tastier results. The trick with squid is to avoid overcooking them or they become rubbery – these rings need no more than a minute's cooking.

SERVES 4
120 ml (4 fl oz/½ cup) dark ale
40g (1½ oz/⅓ cup) plain (all-purpose) flour
salt and freshly ground black pepper
3 whole squid, cleaned
vegetable oil for deep-frying
tarator sauce (page 94) to serve

Make a batter by whisking together the beer and flour. Season lightly with a little salt and pepper.

Rinse the squid and pat dry with paper towel. Cut off the tentacles and reserve. Slice the body into rings about 2 cm (¾ in) wide.

Heat the oil for deep-frying. When it's shimmering, carefully drop a tiny bit of the batter into the oil. If it floats, bubbles and browns immediately, the oil is hot enough. Turn the heat down to medium.

Dip the squid rings and tentacles, one at a time, in the batter, drain off excess and lower into the hot oil in batches. Deep-fry for 1 minute – or less – until golden brown. Remove with a slotted spoon and drain briefly on paper towels before serving hot with tarator sauce.

Kağıtta Levrek

Sea Bass Baked in Paper

Above the Spice Market in Eminou sits a beautiful turquoise-tiled restaurant called Pandeli, founded in 1901. One of their most famous dishes is *kağıtta levrek*: sea bass, herbs and raki wrapped in paper and then baked. This is my version, which I cook when I want to remind myself of sitting in one of their sunny window seats, looking out at the Bosphorous. Don't worry if you don't have raki in the cupboard; you can use any aniseed spirit (I often use absinthe). If you don't like the taste of aniseed, use white wine instead.

SERVES 2
2 sea bass fillets
1 tablespoon olive oil
1 ripe tomato, deseeded and chopped
2 teaspoons finely chopped dill
2 teaspoons finely chopped flat-leaf parsley
2 spring onions (scallions), sliced diagonally
1 tablespoon chopped green (bell) pepper
juice of ½ lemon
1 tablespoon raki or other aniseed spirit, or white wine
pul biber or mild chilli flakes (optional)
salt and freshly ground black pepper

Preheat the oven to 200°C (400°F/gas 6). Cut two rectangles of baking paper, roughly 25 × 20 cm (10 × 8 in), or big enough to comfortably enclose a fish fillet.

Rub the olive oil into the sea bass fillets. Place one fillet in the centre of each rectangle, matching its long edges to the long edges of the paper. Scatter half of each of the chopped tomato, dill, parsley, onion and green pepper over each fillet. Pinch the paper up slightly so the liquids won't run off and add half the lemon juice, raki or wine and 1 teaspoon water to each fish. Finish with a pinch of chilli flakes if using, and a little salt and pepper over each one.

To seal the paper parcels, bring the long edges of the paper together in the middle, above the fish. Fold both edges down, about 1 cm (½ in). Continue to fold the paper over on itself a couple more times until the fold is touching the fish. Fold the loose ends in over themselves several times to seal in the steam. Place on a baking tray and bake for 20 minutes. Serve the fish wrapped in its paper on the plate and let diners release the scented steam themselves.

Mahmudiye

Chicken with Apricots and Almonds

This is an old Ottoman dish – you can tell because of the number of different spices, and the addition of dried fruit and nuts – which has an incredible, intense fragrance as it cooks. I like to make it with orzo, a barley grain-shaped pasta, known as *arpa şehriye* in Turkey. However, you can omit the orzo and serve it with rice or pilaf on the side instead. I find that chicken leg or thigh meat is tastiest, but you can also use breast. As it is quite rich and almost sweet, a green salad with a sharp dressing is a nice accompaniment.

SERVES 4

60 g (2 oz/⅓ cup) stoned dried apricots
1 tablespoon currants
20 g (¾ oz/1½ tablespoons) butter
¼ onion, finely chopped
150 g (5 oz) shallots, peeled but left whole
½ teaspoon salt
600 g (1 lb 5 oz) chicken thigh or leg, bones removed
¼ teaspoon ground cinnamon
2 tablespoons lemon juice
1 teaspoon freshly ground black pepper
700 ml (22 fl oz/2¾ cups) hot chicken stock
50 g (2 oz/generous ½ cup) flaked (slivered) almonds
80 g (3 oz/⅓ cup) orzo

Soak the apricots and currants in boiling water for 10 minutes. Drain and slice each apricot into 2 or 3 pieces. Melt the butter in a large pan with a lid and add the chopped onion and whole shallots. Cook for 10 minutes, stirring, and allow to soften and slightly brown. Add the salt.

Cut the chicken into 5 cm (2 in) pieces, removing most of the skin. Add to the pan and brown gently. Once the chicken has taken on a golden colour all over, add the cinnamon, lemon juice and black pepper. Cook together for 5 minutes, then add the hot stock and dried fruits. Bring to the boil then lower the heat and simmer for 45 minutes with the lid on, stirring occasionally to prevent sticking.

Check the chicken is tender – cook for a little longer if not. If there is a lot of liquid, reduce with the lid off. Toast the almonds very gently in a dry pan until just golden. Tip out of the pan immediately. Add the orzo to the chicken and cook for 3 minutes or until the pasta is just cooked. Serve scattered with the toasted almonds.

Ciğ Balık

Raw Sea Bream Cured in Lemon and Onion

This is another dish I first tried during a day trip to the Prince's Islands, an idyllic car-free island group 11 miles by ferry from Istanbul. From the tiny port, we travelled to a seaside restaurant by *phaeton*, a horse-drawn cart.

COOK'S TIP:
Be sure the fish is as fresh as can be, with clear eyes and red gills. Pre-cut fish from a supermarket isn't suitable for this recipe.

SERVES 4
2 fillets from a whole, very fresh sea bream
¼ onion, very finely sliced into rings
½ teaspoon salt
juice of ½ lemon

Using a very sharp knife at a 45° angle, cut the fish into thin slices. Sprinkle the onion with a pinch of the salt and rub it into the flesh with your finger-tips. Mix the onion and the rest of the salt into the lemon juice.

Lay the fish slices on a plate and pour over the salt/lemon juice mixture and the onions. Mix gently. Place in the fridge for 20 minutes, then take out and gently turn the fish over, ensuring every cut surface of the fish is in contact with the juice. Return to the fridge for 20–30 minutes. Transfer to a clean bowl to serve when the fish is just opaque.

Barbeküde Baharatlı Tavuk

Barbecued Chicken with Sumac

Sumac's sharp lemony flavour is a perfect match for chicken. If you are not confident spatchcocking the chicken – though it is not difficult following my steps below – ask the butcher to do it for you. You could do the same recipe with 2–4 spatchcocked poussins but they will cook in 35–40 minutes maximum.

SERVES 4–6
1 medium chicken

For the marinade:
2 garlic cloves, finely chopped
¼ teaspoon ground cloves
2 tablespoons sumac
¼ teaspoon pul biber or mild chilli flakes
¼ teaspoon salt
grated zest and juice of ½ lemon
½ tablespoon freshly ground black pepper
2 tablespoons olive oil

cucumber and walnut salad (page 68), wilted bitter rocket with chilli (page 188) and garlic yoghurt or cacık (page 62) to serve

With the chicken upside down, so that the breast is facing down, using sturdy scissors or poultry shears, cut along the backbone and through the ribs on both sides and remove it. Then, turn the chicken over and flatten it out with the heel of your hand, so that the breasts are in the centre and facing upwards. If you like, you can use two long metal skewers, threaded diagonally across the chicken in an 'X' shape, to hold it flat while cooking.

Mix the marinade ingredients together in a large bowl. Add the chicken and smear the marinade thoroughly all over the bird. Leave to marinate in the fridge for at least two hours and preferably six, or overnight.

Light the barbecue. When the flames have died down, the coals are white and it is ready to cook on, lower the grill so that is close to the coals and brown the chicken on all sides, until it has a good colour all over. Then raise the grill (or raise the chicken off the grill by about 10 cm/4 in) and cover with a lid (or cover with foil). Allow the chicken to cook slowly, covered, for 45–50 minutes, turning two or three times to ensure even cooking and prevent burning. Pierce the thigh at its thickest point to check if cooked through – the juices should run clear.

Alternatively, brown the marinated chicken all over in a large frying pan, then cook in a preheated oven at 180°C (350°F/gas 4) for 50 minutes, turning once or twice. Serve with cucumber and walnut salad, wilted bitter rocket with chilli, and some garlic yoghurt or cacık.

Asma Yaprağında Sardalya

Sardines Wrapped in Vine Leaves

Preserved vine leaves are a staple of Turkish cooking and wrapping fish in them is a great way to protect the flesh from the direct heat of a grill or barbecue. The richness of sardines is matched nicely by the salty sharpness of the leaves. I like to eat the leaves with the fish, so I rinse and then blanch them to remove much of the salt and brine, but some Turkish people prefer to use them without blanching and to then discard the leaves, allowing the salt to season the fish. In Turkish markets barrels filled with vine leaves stand in rows, each with different levels of salt for use in different dishes: the saltiest leaves have a frosty white crust all over them. In the UK, you can buy them in jars or vacuum-packed.

COOK'S TIP:
When choosing sardines, get ones that smell fresh and preferably without any red bruising around the heads.

SERVES 2-6
12 brined vine leaves
6 fresh sardines, scaled and gutted but with heads on
juice of 1 lemon
1 tablespoon olive oil
freshly ground black pepper
spiced potatoes (page 196) and a tomato salad (page 102) to serve

Rinse the vine leaves and then blanch them in boiling water for 5 minutes. Drain and refresh in cold water. Marinate the fish in the lemon juice, olive oil and black pepper for 5-10 minutes.

Meanwhile, brush a griddle pan or frying pan with oil and place it over a high heat. Wrap each fish in one or two leaves, depending on their size, allowing the heads and tails to poke out. Cook each fish for about 4 minutes each side – if they are particularly fat they may need longer to cook through. Lower the heat if they are cooking too fast on the outside.

The fish are ready when the flesh is just flaking off the bone. Serve straight away with spiced potatoes (page 196) and a tomato salad (page 102).

Karnıyarık

Aubergines Stuffed with Lamb

I first tried this in an *esnaf lokanta*, one of Istanbul's ubiquitous cafés for local workers serving home-style hot dishes, in the Fatih district. We didn't know enough Turkish to order, so ended up pointing and smiling at a few of the dishes bubbling away on the counter. This was one of them and it made a very satisfying lunch.

SERVES 2–4

2 aubergines (eggplants) or 6–8 baby aubergines (depending on how
    small they are)
½ onion, grated
1 garlic clove, finely sliced
15 g (½ oz/1 tablespoon) butter
2 large tomatoes, peeled (blanch in boiling water to make this easier),
    deseeded and chopped
1 tablespoon Turkish tomato paste or tomato purée (paste)
1 tablespoon Turkish red pepper paste, optional (page 214)
250 g (9 oz/generous 1 cup) minced (ground) lamb
1 teaspoon pul biber or mild chilli flakes
¼ teaspoon ground cumin
3 tablespoons roughly chopped flat-leaf parsley
1 teaspoon chopped dill (optional)
50 ml (2 fl oz/¼ cup) stock or water
splash of vegetable oil
1 small, long green pepper, deseeded and diagonally sliced (or ½ green
    (bell) pepper, deseeded and finely sliced)
salad and bread to serve

Halve the aubergines lengthways, keeping the skin on. Run a knife down the middle of the flesh from end to end, but don't cut all the way through to the skin (this helps the aubergine halves open out as they cook). Salt them lightly and drain in a colander for 15 minutes. Rinse and pat dry with paper towels.

Sauté the onion and garlic gently in the butter in a large frying pan for about 3 minutes. Then add the tomatoes, tomato paste and pepper paste, if using. Cook gently for 5 minutes.

Push the tomatoes to the side of the pan and brown the lamb with the spices (use a separate pan if yours isn't big enough for this – if you over-crowd the pan the lamb will stew rather than brown) for about 5 minutes.

Mix the contents of the pan together and season with pepper, but wait until everything has cooked through to taste and add salt, as some brands of tomato and pepper paste can be salty already. Add the parsley, dill, if using, and stock or water and simmer for 10 minutes.

Meanwhile, preheat the oven to 160°C (320°F/gas 3). In a separate frying pan, brown the aubergines in the vegetable oil over a high heat and on all sides. Do this in batches if necessary and be careful as they may spit. The aubergine halves will begin to open up.

Once lightly browned, lay the aubergine halves, cut side up, in a buttered casserole. Top each half with filling – a spoonful or two if they are baby aubergines, more if they are larger. Pull the aubergines apart gently and push the stuffing down to help it sink into the flesh. Toss the pepper slices in a little oil and place one on the top of each aubergine half.

Bake in the oven for 20–30 minutes, until the aubergines are soft and collapsing and the topping is lightly browned. If you're using baby aubergines, check them after 15 minutes, as they may cook much faster. Serve with salad and a little bread to mop up the sauce.

Tantuni

Tantuni-style Wraps

These wraps are late-night favourites in Istanbul, where piles of ready cooked meat (beef or sometimes lamb) are set out each night, waiting to be reheated, spiced and tucked into breads, along with piles of herbs, onion and mint. I prefer to cook the steak through as they often do, but you can also serve it with rare steak strips, rather than cooking it slightly first.

SERVES 2–4
½ onion, very finely sliced
¼ teaspoon salt
5 tablespoons roughly chopped flat-leaf parsley
2 teaspoons sumac (optional)
3 tablespoons mint leaves
4 fresh lavas (page 40), 4 pitta pockets, 4 tortilla wraps or 4 chunks of white baguette, split open
1 x 300 g (10½ oz) beef steak or minced (ground) lamb
1 teaspoon ground cumin
knob of butter
2 juicy tomatoes, deseeded and finely chopped
3 tablespoons hot water
lemon for squeezing over to serve
salt and freshly ground black pepper
plain Turkish or Greek-style yoghurt and pickled chillies (optional)

Mix the onion, salt, parsley, sumac (if using) and mint together in a bowl and set aside. Warm the breads under a medium heat in the grill (broiler).

Cook the steak briefly over a very high heat so that it caramelises on the outside and is blue to rare inside, then slice it into thin strips. (If using lamb, thoroughly brown the mince.)

Return the meat to the very hot pan and add the cumin and butter. Fry over a high heat for 1 minute and then add half of the chopped fresh tomatoes, salt and pepper and the hot water. Cook for 1 minute more, stirring.

Pile each of the breads with a quarter of the meat and a good splash of the pan juices. Add a handful of the onion and herb mixture, a squeeze of lemon and a scattering of the remaining fresh tomatoes. Wrap up and eat immediately. Add a dollop of yoghurt and pickled green chillies, if you like.

Tavuk Kanat

Sticky Chicken Wings

One night, a chef friend took us out for chicken wings: he drove us for an hour, deep into the suburbs of Istanbul, while we wondered where he could be taking us. We found ourselves at an open-air restaurant, Meşhur Kanatçı Haydar'in Yeri, in Yenibosna, where tables of families were busy demolishing huge platters of chicken wings, served with shepherd's salad (page 112) and grilled long green peppers (page 210). The only other thing you'll need is piles and piles of napkins … and, maybe, a cold beer.

SERVES 4–6
20 chicken wings
4 tablespoons hot Turkish red pepper paste (page 214)
½ teaspoon freshly ground black pepper
4 tablespoons olive oil
salt
4 garlic cloves, lightly crushed but whole
1 teaspoon ground cumin
olive oil for frying
salad and bread to serve

Mix all the ingredients together, except the oil, in a large bowl. Place in the fridge to marinade for a couple of hours. Preheat the oven to 230°C (450°F/gas 9). Heat a little oil in a large pan over a high heat and brown the wings all over. Do this in batches of 3 or 4 at a time otherwise they will stew rather than brown.

Arrange the wings in a single layer in a roasting tin. Cook for 10 minutes then reduce the heat to 200°C (400°F/gas 6) and cook for a further 15–25 minutes until the wings are crispy, brown and cooked through (exact cooking time will vary depending on the size of the wings). Turn them halfway through cooking if they're browning too fast.

To check they're cooked through, pierce the fattest part of a wing down to the bone – it should feel really tender and the juices should run clear.

Hamsi Tava

Deep-fried Anchovies or Sprats

Hamsi are a particular favourite of the people living in and around Istanbul. This is how they are most often prepared. I usually use sprats, as fresh anchovies can be hard get hold of in the UK. They are slightly more boney than anchovies, as they are bigger, but just as tasty.

SERVES 4
20 fresh anchovies or 10–12 sprats
60 g (2 oz/½ cup) plain (all-purpose) flour
salt and freshly ground black pepper
vegetable oil for deep-frying
lemon wedges to serve

Heat the oil for deep-frying until a cube of day-old bread sizzles and browns in 30 seconds. Next, put the flour onto a plate and season it generously. Dredge each fish in the flour, ensuring the whole surface gets a dusting, and gently shake off any excess.

Carefully lower the fish into the oil, in batches. Deep- fry for 2 minutes until lightly golden brown and the fish is cooked through. Remove from the oil with a slotted spoon and drain on paper towels. Keep warm while cooking the remaining fish. Serve piping hot with plenty of lemon wedges to squeeze over the fish.

Fresh fish arrives day and night in Istanbul, from the Bosphorus strait, the nearby Black Sea or the Sea of Marmara. Locals even fish along the Golden Horn inlet, landing their catch in buckets of cool water, to take home and cook for supper.

Midye Dolma

Pilaf-stuffed Mussels

Mussel sellers are a fixture on the streets of Istanbul, sitting next to trays of cooked mussels stuffed with spiced rice pilaf. For just a few lira, you get a plump, orange mussel sitting in its shell; snap off the top half, squeeze some lemon juice over the mussel and rice in the bottom and use the top shell as a spoon to scoop out the filling.

SERVES 4 as a hot meze or starter
24 large mussels
100 g (3½ oz/½ cup) long-grain rice
20 g (¾ oz/1½ tablespoons) butter
½ onion, finely chopped
1 tablespoon pine nuts (pine kernels)
1 garlic clove, finely chopped
¼ teaspoon salt
1 teaspoon ground cinnamon
1 teaspoon grated nutmeg
1 teaspoon ground allspice
1 tablespoon currants
1 teaspoon finely chopped dill
1 teaspoon finely chopped flat-leaf parsley
200 ml (7 fl oz/scant 1 cup) hot water, plus a little more to steam
    the mussels
lemon wedges to serve

Scrub and de-beard the mussels. Discard any that do not close if you tap them firmly, or have broken shells. Wash the rice in three changes of water, then cover with fresh cold water and soak for 30 minutes.

Meanwhile, melt the butter in a lidded pan large enough to cook the rice in and gently fry the onion, pine nuts and garlic with the salt for 5 minutes, stirring. Add the spices and cook for a further 2 minutes. Drain the soaked rice and add to the pan with the currants – cook, stirring, for 1–2 minutes, until the rice is fully coated in the butter. Add the hot water, bring to the boil, reduce the heat as low as possible, cover tightly with a lid and simmer for 10 minutes. Remove from the heat and stir in the dill and parsley.

In a large pan, big enough to hold all the mussels, bring about 1 cm (½ in) water to the boil over a high heat. Put the mussels into the pan, clamp a lid on and steam for 2–3 minutes. Remove the lid and drain the mussels. Discard any that have not opened. Set the pan back over the heat with the

MEAT AND FISH

same amount of boiling water in again. Working quickly but carefully, because both the mussels and rice will be hot, stuff each mussel with a tablespoon or two of the rice mixture. Wipe any excess off the outside of the shell and gently press the two halves together – they won't entirely close.

Tuck the filled mussels tightly into a metal colander or a steamer and set over the boiling pan of water. Cover and steam for 3 minutes. Remove from the heat and transfer to a bowl or individual plates. Serve piping hot with plenty of lemon wedges to squeeze over.

Tavuklu Pilav

Fragrant Chicken Pilaf

Pilaf is a hugely important dish in Istanbul – so much so that you can find pilaf carts on street corners, serving up takeaway bowls of fluffy white rice, studded with pine nuts (pine kernels) or chickpeas (garbanzos). There are as many variations on it as there are cooks in Istanbul: it can come with nuts, fish or meat, or flavoured with saffron or spices. But on one point everyone is clear: you must never serve wet, sticky rice. Thankfully it's easy to avoid this (see my tip below). Pilaf can also be made with burghul (bulgur) wheat and both kinds can be used to stuff meat or vegetables. This recipe a great way to use up the leftovers from a roast chicken and makes a lovely Monday night supper.

COOK'S TIP:
For perfect, fluffy rice, wash it in several changes of water, and then soak in cold water for 30 minutes before cooking (although 10 minutes will more or less do the trick if you're short of time). Soaking also shortens the cooking time.

SERVES 2
150 g (5 oz/⅔ cup) long-grain rice
40 g (1½ oz/3 tablespoons) butter
2 tablespoons pine nuts (pine kernels)
1 onion, finely chopped
salt to taste
1 garlic clove, finely chopped
¼ teaspoon freshly ground black pepper
¼ teaspoon ground cinnamon
¼ teaspoon ground allspice
2 tablespoons currants
300 ml (10 fl oz/1¼ cups) hot stock (preferably chicken or vegetable)
400 g (14 oz) cooked chicken, skin on, torn into bite-sized pieces
lemon juice
plain Turkish or Greek-style yoghurt to serve (optional)

Wash the rice in three changes of water, then soak in cold water for 30 minutes. Melt the butter in a large saucepan with a lid. Toast the pine nuts gently, stirring to prevent burning. Scatter a pinch of salt over the onion and mix together. Add the onion and garlic to the pan and soften in the butter for 5–6 minutes, stirring.

Drain the washed and soaked rice and add it to the pan. Stir to coat the rice with the butter and allow to absorb for a minute or two. Add a generous pinch of salt plus all the spices and the currants. Stir to combine and then add the hot stock. Bring to the boil and cover tightly with the lid. Reduce the heat as low as possible and simmer for 8–10 minutes, until the rice is almost cooked.

Gently stir through the pieces of chicken. Cover and heat through for a couple of minutes until piping hot. Remove from the heat and leave to stand for 5 minutes, with the lid on again. Before serving, fluff the rice up with a fork, squeeze over a little lemon juice and serve. This is great with a dollop of yoghurt on the side.

Barbunya Tava

Fried Red Mullet with Herbed Pilaf

The soft and fragrant green herbs in this simple pilaf match perfectly with the hot, crisp-skinned red mullet. At Istanbul's many fish restaurants, often you will be led up to the fish counter to choose a perfectly fresh fish for your supper – gleaming red mullet piled next to silver anchovies, horse mackerel, blue fish, sardines, bass and bream.

SERVES 2

For the pilaf:
150 g (5 oz/⅔ cup) long-grain rice
40 g (1½ oz/3 tablespoons) butter
3 tablespoons pine nuts (pine kernels)
1 onion, finely chopped
salt to taste
1 garlic clove, finely chopped
¼ teaspoon freshly ground black pepper
300 ml (10 fl oz/1¼ cups) hot vegetable stock or water
1 tablespoon finely chopped dill
2 tablespoons finely chopped flat-leaf parsley
2 spring onions (scallions), sliced into thin rounds
1 teaspoon lemon juice (or to taste)

For the red mullet:
1 or 2 whole red mullet per person, gutted and cleaned
vegetable oil for deep-frying
2–4 tablespoons plain (all-purpose) flour
salt and freshly ground black pepper
lemon wedges to serve

Wash the rice in three changes of water, then soak in fresh, cold water for 30 minutes. Melt the butter in a large saucepan with a lid. Toast the pine nuts gently, stirring to prevent burning. Scatter a pinch of salt over the onions and mix together. Add the onion and garlic to the pan and soften in the butter for 5–6 minutes, stirring.

Drain the rice and add it to the pan. Stir to coat the rice with the butter and allow to absorb for 1–2 minutes. Add a generous pinch of salt and the black pepper. Stir to combine and then add the hot stock. Bring to the boil and cover tightly with the lid. Reduce the heat as low as possible and simmer for 8–10 minutes, until the rice is just cooked.

Remove the rice from the heat and add the herbs and spring onions. Stir once and then leave to stand for 5 minutes, with the lid on again.

Meanwhile, to cook the fish, heat the oil for deep-frying until a cube of day-old bread sizzles and browns in 30 seconds. Put the flour on a plate and season it generously. Dredge the fish in the flour, ensuring the whole surface gets a dusting, and gently shake off any excess. Carefully lower the fish into the oil, in twos or one at a time. Deep-fry for 4–6 minutes, depending on the size of the fish. Remove from the oil and drain on paper towels. (To check the fish is cooked through, insert a sharp knife into the fish by the spine. If the fish is flaking and no longer translucent, it is cooked.) Serve the fish on top of a heap of the fluffy, herbed rice, with lemon wedges to squeeze over.

Fırında Hamsi

Tray-baked Anchovies

This recipe works for all sorts of small fish as fresh anchovies can be hard to find. Here, I've done it with sprats, but you could use herrings, sardines, even mackerel, or fillets of white fish.

COOK'S TIP:
You can fillet anchovies and sprats if you'd like to serve them without bones in: find the lower fin at the base of the belly of the fish and gently pull off. Run your thumb up from the hole this creates towards the head and remove the guts. Twist off the head and then find the top of the spine and push your thumb underneath it. Run your thumb down the fish, under the spine towards the tail, and the bones will easily come out. Leave the two fillets together, as though butterflied, and cook as below. They will cook quickly, so be vigilant.

SERVES 4
½ onion, sliced into half moons
3 tablespoons roughly chopped flat-leaf parsley
3 tablespoons Turkish tomato paste or concentrated tomato purée
   (paste)
1 lemon, sliced into wedges
4 tablespoons olive oil
1 red chilli, deseeded and finely sliced
8 cherry tomatoes, halved, or 1 large tomato cut into wedges
¼ teaspoon sumac
16 stoned black olives
lots of salt and freshly ground black pepper
1 kg (2lb 3 oz) sprats, anchovies or other small oily fish, rinsed and
   patted dry with paper towel
a green salad, wilted rocket (page 188) or garlic samphire
   (page 192) and bread to serve

Preheat the oven to 180°C (350°F/gas 4). Soften the onion in a little olive oil for 5 minutes. Tip into a large baking tin and add all the other ingredients except the fish. Mix thoroughly then add the fish and gently mix, to ensure they are all well-coated. Spread out in a single layer and bake for 15 minutes. Meanwhile preheat the grill (broiler). When the fish is cooked, place the dish or tin under the grill for a few minutes to brown. Serve with salad and plenty of bread.

SEBZE YEMEKLERİ

Vegetables and Sides

The fertile Turkish country-side supplies wonderful vegetables to Istanbul, and local markets are always piled high with seasonal ingredients. Try cooking vegetables like green beans or leeks slowly in olive oil, or try bitter greens wilted with chilli as a side to grilled. Pilaf is a vital Turkish dish, served as a main or side (or midnight snack from tiny stalls with striped red awnings).

Kuru Fasulye

White Beans in Tomato Sauce

This is a much-loved dish in Istanbul and across Turkey: steaming bowls appear on the lunch counters of *esnaf lokantasi* – cafés serving home-style food all over the city. Some say that the clay pot it is sometimes cooked in influences the flavour, others that it's all about the chef manning the stove. You'll find it made with meat – slow-cooked nuggets of lamb, chunks of chicken, slices of rich beef *sucuk* sausage – stewed with vegetables or served plain: the sauce almost a tomato broth. Traditionally it is eaten with fluffy rice and, maybe, some pickled vegetables. Try adding meat to this basic recipe, or cubes of fried aubergine (eggplant). If you prefer to use dried beans, rather than canned, soak 115g (4 oz/generous ½ cup) in plenty of water overnight, then boil rapidly in plenty of water (without salt), for 10 minutes, then simmer until tender but not mushy, about 1 hour.

SERVES 2–3
1 onion, finely chopped
½ green (bell) pepper, deseeded and sliced into strips
20 g (¾oz/1½ tablespoons) butter
1 tablespoon Turkish tomato paste or concentrated tomato
    purée (paste)
1 teaspoon red pepper paste, optional (page 214)
1 large fresh tomato, skinned, deseeded and diced
pinch of cumin seeds
300 ml (10 fl oz/1¼ cups) hot water
400 g (14 oz) can of cannellini or other white beans, drained and
    rinsed
salt and freshly ground black pepper
rice or crusty bread to serve

Soften the onion and pepper in the butter in a large pan over a low heat, stirring. After about 10 minutes, add the tomato and pepper pastes. Cook for 2 minutes, stirring, and then add the fresh tomato. Allow to cook for a further 2–3 minutes.

Meanwhile toast the cumin seeds in a dry pan, just until fragrant. Grind them to a powder in a pestle and mortar and add to the tomato and onion mixture. Add the hot water to the pan and bring to the boil. Add the cannellini beans. Simmer everything, stirring occasionally, until the sauce has reduced to a thick soupy consistency, about 15 minutes. Taste and add a little seasoning. Serve with rice or crusty bread.

In Istanbul's many, many street markets, people jostle each other for the freshest, ripest fruit and vegetables. Everyone has a favourite vendor – the best place for green herbs, the perfect spot for tomatoes. Follow a local doing her daily shop and you'll discover the best stalls too.

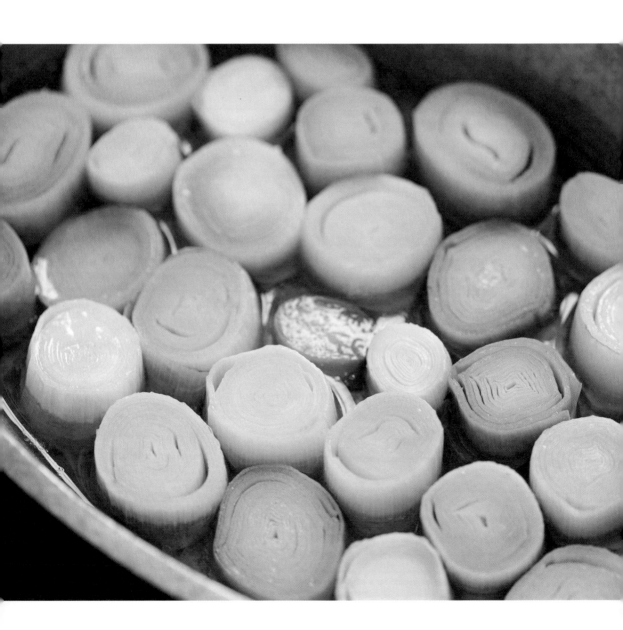

Zeytinyağlı Pırasa

Leeks Slow-cooked in Olive Oil

There is a whole group of Turkish dishes known as *zeytinyağli* dishes, which means both 'olive oil' and 'cooked in olive oil', and this is just one of the vegetables you can treat this way. Root vegetables, green beans (page 199), brassicas and leafy greens can all be cooked submerged in olive oil – long and slow, separately or mixed together. Plainer, less flavoursome vegetables are often cooked with carrots, onions and tomatoes in the same dish. They can come as a surprise to those of us who like vegetables just-cooked and crisp, but cooking vegetables this way turns them into comforting, silky dishes. Zeytinyağli dishes are mostly served cool, not hot, but I like them warm as well as chilled, too. You can also add the chopped leaves from a sprig or two of coarse herbs like thyme or rosemary to the braise, or add soft ones, like parsley, oregano or dill at the end, if you like.

SERVES 4
5 leeks
120 ml (4 fl oz/½ cup) olive oil
¼ teaspoon salt
lemon juice to serve

Preheat the oven to 160°C (320°F/gas 3). Remove the base and green tops of the leeks, plus the tough outer first and second layers. Slice each leek into 2.5 cm (1 in) pieces. Rinse away any soil. Place the rounds standing up in an ovenproof baking dish, preferably with a lid.

Pour over the olive oil, add 3 tablespoons water and sprinkle on the salt (if you are adding coarse herbs, do so now). Cover with a lid or tightly with foil and place in the oven. Cook for 1 hour or until the leeks are meltingly soft.

Leave to cool slightly in the olive oil then lift out and serve with a little lemon juice. Serve either warm with fish dishes or lamb chops, or cool as part of a meze.

Roka Salatası

Warm Bitter Rocket

We're often served bowls of wilted bitter greens like dandelions in our favourite Istanbul restaurants and, back in London, rocket (arugula) is a good substitute. Cooking enhances its strong, sharp and peppery notes.

SERVES 4
300 g (10½ oz) rocket (arugula)
knob of butter
1 fresh red chilli (or to taste), deseeded and finely chopped
1 teaspoon lemon juice
salt and freshly ground black pepper

Wash the rocket and shake off excess moisture. Melt the butter in a large saucepan set over a medium heat. When the butter is foaming, add the wet rocket. Stir until wilted – this will take just a couple of minutes. Remove from the heat, drain the liquid from the pan, and add the chilli, lemon juice and a little salt and pepper. Serve hot alongside meat or fish.

Pirinçli Ispanak

Rice and Spinach

You'll see this dish on steaming lunch counters all over the city. Although it can be a main course in its own right for a couple of people, it's lovely with grilled lamb chops. Sprinkling onion with salt before frying helps it release its juices and prevents browning when cooking.

SERVES 4
1 onion, halved and sliced into thin half moons
salt and freshly ground black pepper
80 g (3 oz/generous ⅓ cup) long-grain rice
350 g (12 oz) fresh spinach leaves
1 tablespoon olive oil
3 garlic cloves (or to taste), thinly sliced
1 tablespoon Turkish tomato paste or concentrated tomato purée (paste)
1 tablespoon hot or mild red pepper paste (page 214), or ½ teaspoon of paprika
1 fresh tomato, peeled, deseeded and chopped
300 ml (10 fl oz/1¼ cups) hot chicken or vegetable stock
plain or garlic yoghurt (page 84) to serve

Sprinkle the sliced onion with a pinch of salt, stir and set aside. Rinse the rice in three changes of water then leave to soak in fresh cold water for 30 minutes. Wash and drain the spinach. If the leaves are large, chop them roughly, and remove any stalks. In a pan set over a medium heat, wilt the spinach gently, stirring and turning. Remove from the pan and drain thoroughly. Allow to cool slightly then roughly chop.

Meanwhile soften the salted onion gently in the olive oil for 10 minutes until it is translucent but not browned. Add the garlic and cook for 3 minutes. Stir in the tomato and pepper pastes and cook for 2–3 minutes, to allow the mixture to caramelise slightly, but not burn.

Add the fresh tomato and cook for a further 2 minutes. Add the rice and hot stock to the pan and bring to the boil. Reduce the heat to low and simmer gently for 15–20 minutes until the rice is tender and has absorbed the liquid, stirring occasionally to prevent sticking. Finally, stir in the cooked spinach. Season to taste and serve with a dollop of plain or garlic yoghurt.

Deniz Börülcesi

Samphire with Garlic

Samphire, also known as glasswort, marsh samphire or pickleweed, is often translated as sea bean in Turkey, which makes sense – it grows in salty coastal areas, and its fronds do look a little like green beans. It can be served as a meze dish but is also lovely served alongside fish. Samphire is in season during the summer months. Look out for bright green fronds and discard any woody stems before cooking.

SERVES 2
150 g (5 oz) samphire
1 teaspoon butter
1 teaspoon olive oil
½ garlic clove, very finely chopped
1 teaspoon lemon juice (or more to taste)

Pick over the samphire and wash it thoroughly under running water in a colander. Melt the butter in a wide pan and add the oil. Add the samphire and garlic and toss in the hot butter and oil mixture.

Cook over a low heat for 1–2 minutes, until hot through. Remove the pan and serve in a warmed bowl, with a squeeze of lemon juice over the top. As samphire grows in salty conditions it won't need more salt.

Tavada Patates Salatası

Spiced Potatoes

These sticky-sweet potatoes make a lovely side dish – have them warm with meat or fish, or room temperature as part of a meze. Don't worry if some of the onions get a little charred during cooking as that adds to the flavour.

SERVES 4

1 onion, halved and sliced into thin half moons
salt and freshly ground black pepper
750 g (1lb 10 oz) waxy potatoes, scrubbed and cut into 2.5 cm (1 in) chunks
5–6 tablespoons olive oil
2 tablespoons Turkish tomato paste or concentrated tomato purée (paste)
2 tablespoons chopped flat-leaf parsley
2–3 teaspoons pul biber or mild chilli flakes
1 tablespoon freshly squeezed lemon juice

Toss the onions with a pinch of salt. Parboil the potatoes for 10–12 minutes, until just tender. Drain and leave to stand a few minutes to dry off.

Heat 2 tablespoons of olive oil in a pan over a low heat and soften the onion for 10 minutes, until translucent but not browned. Add 2–3 more tablespoons of oil and the potatoes. Cook for about 15 minutes or until tender and beginning to turn crisp and golden brown, stirring frequently.

Finally add the tomato paste and cook for a further 3 minutes. To serve, stir in the parsley and chilli flakes and finish with a squeeze of lemon juice and a drizzle of olive oil.

Taze Fasulye

Slow-cooked Green Beans in Olive Oil

If, like me, you love a crisp green bean that has barely touched boiling water, this recipe might not seem like one for you at first. But in this second *zeytinyağli* dish (see the leeks, page 187) the beans are meltingly soft when you finally take the pan off the heat and are packed with flavour. They are often served cold, but I like them warm as well.

SERVES 4
½ onion, finely chopped
100 ml (3½ fl oz/scant ½ cup) olive oil
1 garlic clove, finely sliced
300 g (10½ oz) fine green or French beans, topped and tailed
   if necessary
4 tomatoes, deseeded and finely chopped
juice of ½ lemon
salt and freshly ground black pepper

Gently soften the onion in a little of the olive oil in a large saucepan with a lid, until translucent but not browned, about 10 minutes. Add the rest of the oil, the garlic, beans, tomatoes, lemon juice, lots of salt and black pepper, and stir briefly.

Add just enough water to cover, bring to the boil, turn down to a gentle simmer and cover with a lid. Simmer for at least 1 hour, until the beans are falling apart, and longer if necessary. Remove the lid for the last 15 minutes or so to allow the liquid to reduce a little, but don't let it dry out. Serve cold as part of a meze or warm as a side dish.

Pilav

Plain Pilaf

Serve this basic pilaf as a side dish, or add seasonal or your favourite ingredients to make it a main meal: you can add peas and green beans alongside soft green herbs like parsley, dill or even mint; pulses like cooked chickpeas (garbanzo beans); sautéed vegetables like aubergine (eggplant); (bell) peppers or courgettes (zucchini); and spices like saffron, allspice or cinnamon.

SERVES 4 as a side dish
½ onion, finely chopped
salt
150 g (5 oz/¾ cup) long-grain rice
30 g (1 oz/2 tablespoons) butter
2 tablespoons pine nuts (pine kernels)
300 ml (10 fl oz/1½ cups) hot chicken or vegetable stock

Sprinkle the onion with a pinch of salt, stir and set aside. Rinse the rice in three changes of water, then soak in clean cold water for 30 minutes.

Melt the butter in a large saucepan with a lid. Toast the pine nuts gently, stirring to prevent burning. Immediately tip out of the pan onto a plate. Add the salted onion to the pan and soften in the butter very gently for 5–6 minutes, stirring until soft but not brown.

Drain the rice and add it to the pan. Stir thoroughly to coat the rice with the butter and allow to absorb for a minute or two. Add the hot stock and bring to the boil and cover tightly with a lid. Reduce the heat to low and simmer gently for 8–10 minutes, or until the rice is just cooked and has absorbed the liquid.

Remove the rice from the heat and stir once. Re-cover and leave to stand for 5 minutes. Fluff up with a fork and serve immediately.

Kırmızı Lahana Salatası

Red Cabbage Salad

With its fresh, sharp flavour and crunchy texture, this vibrant, almost pickled cabbage salad works brilliantly as an accompaniment to kebabs or rich slow-cooked meats.

SERVES 4
½ head red cabbage
1 teaspoon fine salt
1 teaspoon freshly squeezed lemon juice

Finely shred the cabbage, discarding the thick central stalk. Sprinkle with the salt and toss thoroughly to combine. Place it all in a colander to drain for 30 minutes. The salt will penetrate the cabbage, remove moisture and slightly soften it.

Rinse thoroughly then squeeze the water from the cabbage, using your hands. Rinse again and allow to drain for a minute or two. At this point the cabbage will be a blueish purple. Tip into a bowl, then squeeze over the lemon juice and toss – the lemon will turn the cabbage closer to dark pink. Taste and add more lemon juice if you prefer a sharper flavour.

Kısır

Burghul Wheat Salad

This sharp-tasting, orange-coloured wheat dish often appears as part of a meze on restaurant tables across Istanbul. Every cook makes it differently, depending on where in Turkey they come from: some add crisp lettuce and chopped cucumber; others make it with dried mint or fresh dill. Treat this is as the base recipe and experiment with different ingredients. It's not dissimilar to tabbouleh and is great as a side to cooked meats or as a hearty salad. If you don't have Turkish tomato paste or red pepper paste you won't get the bright colour, but don't worry, just add extra fresh tomato and perhaps half a finely diced red (bell) pepper.

SERVES 4
250 g (9 oz/1½ cups) burghul (bulgur) wheat
3 tablespoons Turkish tomato paste
½ onion, very finely chopped
1 tablespoon hot or mild red pepper paste (page 214)
1 small spring onion (scallion), very finely chopped
1 tablespoon pomegranate molasses or the juice of ½ lemon
2 tablespoons olive oil
2 tablespoons finely chopped mint leaves
1 large tomato, deseeded and finely chopped
2 tablespoons (finely chopped) flat-leaf parsley
pul biber or mild chilli flakes (optional)

Cook or rehydrate the burghul wheat according to the packet instructions and taste to check it is not still hard and grainy (I usually cover it with boiling water and leave for 15–20 minutes, then fluff up with a fork).

When cool enough to handle, add the tomato paste, pepper paste and onion and gently rub everything together with your hands until it is thoroughly combined and an even red-orange colour. Add all the other ingredients and mix thoroughly again. Taste and season, if necessary. Add more olive oil, pomegranate molasses or lemon juice too, if you like. Chill for 30 minutes before serving (if you have time).

ÇEŞNİ

Pickles and Garnishes

Turkish food is almost always served with garnishes, like little bowls of flaked chilli pepper. But other extra flavours are also much loved, like the mild green peppers that are grilled and served with meat, or the white onions that are salted and dusted with *sumac* to go in wraps, alongside kebabs or with chops. Even more important are the sharp-sweet pickles, served with rice, vegetables or even alone, and the deeply flavoured red pepper paste, used in every possible dish.

Sivri Biber

Grilled Long Green Peppers

Although we associate hot, pickled, thin green chilli peppers with kebabs, in Istanbul meat is just as often served with grilled or roasted small, long, mild green peppers. Their intense, slightly bitter flavour makes a lovely pairing with meats and fish.

SERVES 4
4 or 8 small, long, mild green peppers
vegetable oil

Heat a griddle pan or frying pan until very hot. Alternatively, set the grill (broiler) to its highest heat. Brush the peppers with just a splash of oil to prevent sticking.

Place the peppers in the pan or under the grill and cook until they just begin to blister and blacken – about five minutes. Turn and do the same to the other side. Remove from the heat. The peppers will begin to collapse slightly but should still have a little texture.

Serve whole or sliced on top of grilled chops, alongside kebabs, in wraps or with simple fish dishes.

Turşu

Turkish-style Pickles

Pickles are an essential part of the Turkish kitchen and there are pickle shops all over Istanbul. Anything that can be pickled is pickled – grapes, quinces, lemons, baby corn cobs, whole heads of garlic, wedges of cabbage – and some locals even pop out for a late-morning cup of pickles and brine. Pickle shops also sell fermented juices – I've tried fermented blackcurrant, which is sweet, fruity and sour and fermented red carrot juice, *şalgam*, which is intensely flavoured and salty. Some people even drink it alongside raki, Turkey's aniseed-flavoured national spirit, to prevent hangovers.

COOK'S TIP:
These pickles will keep for a few months in the fridge and are a delicious counterpoint to rich meat dishes, kebabs or anything served with rice and yoghurt.

MAKES A 1 LITRE (34 fl oz) JAR
600 g (1 lb 5 oz) mixture of any of the following: shallots or baby onions; garlic cloves; baby carrots or sliced whole carrots; sliced fennel; radishes; cauliflower florets; and hot or mild green chilli peppers
500 ml (17 fl oz/2¼ cups) water
50 ml (2 fl oz/¼ cup) cider (apple cider) vinegar
1 tablespoon salt
1 tablespoon caster (superfine) sugar
1 teaspoon coriander seeds

Wash and sterilise a large 1 litre (34 fl oz) jar with a lid. Remove the jar's rubber seal if it has one, and then place in the oven for 30 minutes at 140°C (275°F/gas 1). Wash and prepare the vegetables: peel the onions and garlic and scrub and slice (if necessary) the carrots. Bring a small amount of the water to the boil and blanch the chilli peppers, if using. Keep the water.

Pack all the vegetables into the sterilised jar, pressing them down tightly. Add the rest of the water to the chilli-blanching water and bring to the boil. Mix in the vinegar, salt and sugar and stir to dissolve. Add the coriander seeds and pour the pickling mix into the jar and over the vegetables. (If you find there is not enough, mix a little more vinegar and water together at a ratio of 1:10 vinegar to water.)

Cover, leave to cool, then store in the fridge. Leave for 2–3 weeks to mature. Serve alongside spicy meats, with pilaf or with smoked fish.

Biber Salçası

Quick Red Pepper Paste

Biber Salçası, whether bought in a jar from a Middle Eastern store or tasted in Turkey itself, is a thick red paste with the same texture as concentrated tomato purée (paste). It takes a long time to make and you need a good dose of sunshine to do it properly, as it gets its dark red colour from the paste spending hours drying in the sun. If you can't find ready-made red pepper paste, this is a great substitute and doesn't take as long to make. Keep it in the fridge in a sterilised jar with a layer of oil over the top and it will stay fresh for a couple of weeks.

MAKES 1 JAR about 200 g (7oz/scant 1 cup)
3 red (bell) peppers
2 red chillies (or to taste)
½ teaspoon salt
1 tablespoon caster (superfine) sugar
1 tablespoon olive oil
1 tablespoon white wine vinegar or cider (apple cider) vinegar
vegetable oil

Wash and sterilise a medium-sized glass jar with a lid. Remove the jar's rubber seal if it has one, and then place in the oven for 30 minutes at 140°C (275°F/gas 1).

Scrape the seeds out of the red bell peppers and chillies and remove the membranes from the inside. Place the flesh in a blender or food processor with the rest of the ingredients except the vegetable oil and blitz to a pulp.

Scoop the mixture into a pan set over a medium heat and cook slowly for 30–40 minutes, stirring frequently, until well reduced and you are left with a sticky red paste.

Scrape the hot paste into the sterilised jar. Pour a layer of vegetable oil over the paste to seal it then put the lid on. Keep in the fridge. Taste before using to check its spice levels.

Soğan Salatası

Sumac Onions

Sweet-tasting white onions dusted with sumac make regular appearances on tables around Istanbul. Sprinkled and rubbed with salt, raw onions become soft and almost sweet, a delicious match for lemony sumac, which is easy to find in Middle Eastern stores, some supermarkets or online. The onions are often served alongside a bowl of freshly chopped flat-leaf parsley and pul biber, the lovely mild red chilli flakes locals love to scatter over most dishes.

SERVES 4
1 onion
pinch of salt
½ teaspoon sumac

Cut the onion in half and discard the outer layer (the first one after the papery skin) if it seems tough. Slice the onion into half moons as thinly as possible.

Place the sliced onion in a bowl and add the salt. Mix thoroughly and rub the salt into the flesh, then add the sumac. Let sit for a couple of minutes before serving (but not too long as the onions soak up the colour of the sumac and can look grey after a while).

TATLILAR, PASTALAR VE İÇECEKLER

Desserts, Cakes and Drinks

In Istanbul, there's always time to stop for something sweet, whether for a late night snack, a pudding or a mid-morning treat. On the streets you can buy anything from wedges of melon, sharp green plums and bags of ripe cherries, to boxes of sticky, flaky *baklava*, filled with pistachios. Here you'll find rich semolina cake and traditional sweet pastries and puddings, all perfect with a cup of thick Turkish coffee, or for something fresher, a light melon sorbet.

Kavunlu Sorbet

Melon Sorbet

In the summer, delivery men pull two-wheeled handcarts laden with melons up and down the hills of Istanbul by hand, and you can buy a wedge of cool, juicy watermelon to eat for just a few pence on most street corners. Ice creams and sorbets are sold from stalls dotted all over the city. This dessert is a perfect way to marry up two things that always remind me of Istanbul.

COOK'S TIP:
For this sorbet, you can use any type of melon. Once it's cubed, you can store it in the freezer for several weeks until you're ready to use it.

SERVES 4-6
2 kg (4 lb 6 oz) melon
¼ teaspoon salt (or to taste)
2 teaspoons freshly squeezed lemon juice (or to taste)
3-4 tablespoons caster (superfine) sugar (or to taste)

Cut the melon into wedges and remove the skin and seeds. Chop the flesh into 2 cm (¾ in) chunks. Place on a baking sheet and freeze overnight. Store in a tub or bag if not using immediately after freezing.

The next day, and at least 3 hours before you want to serve the sorbet, place the frozen chunks in a blender and blitz to a purée – you may need to do this in small batches depending on the capacity and strength of your blender. Taste and add the salt, lemon juice and a little sugar, all to taste. Scoop into a plastic box with a lid.

If it seems too stiff, add a splash of water. Whisk with a fork to mix and then return to the freezer for two hours. Remove from the freezer and whisk thoroughly again, then re-freeze for a further hour and serve.

Bülbül Yuvası

Sweet Pistachio Nests

Because they are made with pistachio and sugar syrup, these pastries taste similar to baklava. Baklava makers in Istanbul inspire great debate about their relative merits, and most people have a favourite store – mine is a little spot called Bilgeoğlu in Kadıköy on the Asian side, where they've been making nothing but baklava since 1956. Such is their love of the pastries, some locals can manage a portion of six pieces in one go, as a between-meals snack, but I can't manage more than two. Baklava are notoriously difficult to make, but these nests are much simpler while still looking pretty impressive.

COOK'S TIP:
In Turkey bülbül yuvası are made by wrapping the dough round an *oklava*, a long thin rolling pin. I use a piece of 2 cm (¾ in) wooden dowling, 40 cm (16 in) long but anything similar will do – even a clean piece of old pipe. (See note on dough, page 52)

MAKES 12–14 NESTS
For the sugar syrup:
250 g (9 oz/generous 1 cup) caster (superfine) sugar
1 tablespoon freshly squeezed lemon juice

For the nests:
200 g (7 oz/1⅓ cups) walnut pieces
200 g (7 oz/1⅓ cups) unsalted shelled pistachios
1 tablespoon sugar
75 g (2¾ oz/generous ¼ cup) butter, melted
12–14 sheets rectangular yufka or filo (phyllo) dough
ice cream or clotted cream (optional) to serve

Make the sugar syrup: heat 200 ml (7 fl oz/generous ¾ cup) water with the sugar and lemon juice in a saucepan, stirring until dissolved. Bring to the boil then remove from the heat, cool, and chill until required.

Preheat the oven to 180°C (350°F/gas 4). Mix 165 g (5¼ oz/1¼ cups) of the walnuts, 165 g (5¼ oz/1¼ cups) of the pistachios and the sugar together and blitz in food processor or crush in a pestle and mortar until the mixture resembles rough sand (make sure there are no big chunks of nut which will puncture the pastry and make the coils split). The remaining nuts are for decoration, so crush them more coarsely.

Butter a baking dish approximately 25 × 40 cm (10 × 16 in). Open the packet of pastry and cover the sheets with a damp cloth. Lay a sheet of pastry on a work surface. Brush it lightly with melted butter. Across one of the narrow ends of the sheet, thinly spread a heaped tablespoon of the ground nuts.

Grease your oklava or improvised rolling pin and lay it across that end of the sheet of pastry, in line with the edge. Begin to wrap the pastry around it, enclosing the nuts in a tube. Roll the pin along the whole sheet until all the pastry is wrapped around it. Very gently, push the pastry towards the middle of the pin from either end so that it crinkles and bunches up like a haphazard concertina. Then slowly slide the whole thing off the pin. Tuck one crinkled end in on itself and wrap the rest around in a coil. Place in the baking dish and brush with plenty of melted butter. Repeat to make the remaining coils.

When all of the coils have been made, check that they all have a good glaze of melted butter and then bake in the oven for 25 minutes or until they are golden brown. Remove from the oven and, while they are still hot, pour over the sugar syrup. Allow to cool and then scatter the remaining nuts in the centre of each coil. Serve as an afternoon snack, or with a dollop of ice cream or clotted cream as a dessert.

Künefe

Sweet Ricotta Pudding

This pudding is made with *kadayif*, a kind of shredded pastry. It's often translated as "shredded wheat" but is used so luxuriously, soaked in syrup or coated in butter, that it couldn't be further from the breakfast cereal of the same name. You can buy it in Turkish or Middle Eastern stores, either frozen or fresh and vacuum sealed, and it keeps for ages. It's made by extruding wet raw dough through a mesh and onto hot plates, where it sets in long, thin strands. I like künefe best eaten no more than an hour after it is made, while the sweet cheese centre is still just squidgy.

SERVES 6–8

250 g (9 oz) kadayif shredded pastry (½ packet)

100 g (3½ oz/1 stick less 1 tablespoon) butter, melted and slightly cooled

60 g (2 oz/¼ cup) ricotta

60 g (2 oz/½ cup) buffalo mozzarella, shredded

200 g (7 oz/scant 1 cup) caster (superfine) sugar

thick cream, ice cream or plain Turkish or Greek-style yoghurt to serve (optional)

Grease an 18 cm (7 in) springform cake tin. Preheat the oven to 180°C (350°F/gas 4). Gently pull apart the kadayif, making sure none of the strands have clumped together in sticky or dry lumps (discard any bits that are very soggy). Lay it all on a board – it will form an unruly heap – and, using a sharp knife, repeatedly chop straight through the pile, breaking the strands into rough 2.5 cm (1 in) lengths.

Place the chopped kadayif in a bowl and add the melted butter. Using your hands, mix thoroughly, ensuring all the pastry gets a good coating of butter. Divide the buttered kadayif into two equal amounts. Press one half into the bottom of the cake tin, ensuring it completely covers the base. It should be about 2 cm (¾ in) thick.

Mix the two cheeses together, again using your hands to ensure they are thoroughly combined. Scatter the cheese mixture thinly on top of the layer of kadayif in the cake tin and use a rubber or plastic spatula to push and spread it evenly over the pastry strands, making sure it completely covers the pastry.

Spread the second half of the kadayif over the cheese layer and press it down with your hands, again ensuring the cheese is totally covered. Bake for 1 hour, or until the pastry is crisp and lightly golden brown.

Meanwhile, mix the sugar with 200 ml (7 fl oz/generous ¾ cup) water in a saucepan. Heat gently until dissolved then bring to the boil and boil briskly until the syrup has reduced by a quarter, to about 150 ml (5 fl oz/½ cup). It's ready when it is viscous and coats the back of a spoon. (Unless it becomes fully syrupy, it won't hold the künefe together.) Remove the syrup from the heat and pour into a jug or bowl to cool.

When the künefe is cooked, remove it from the oven and place on a plate, still in its tin. Pour over the cooled syrup. Leave for 10–15 minutes for the pastry to absorb the syrup and for the whole thing to set slightly. Remove the tin. Cut into small wedges to serve, perhaps with some thick cream, ice cream or yoghurt.

Tel Kadayıf

Sweet Pistachio Pastries

This dessert is made in the same way as Künefe (page 226), but with ground nuts inside rather than cheese. I like to scatter freshly ground pistachios over the top as I love the contrast between the roasty flavours of the nuts in the middle, and the bright green nuts on top. Tel Kadayif is lovely as a dessert with thick cream, ice cream or yoghurt, or on its own as an afternoon treat.

SERVES 6–8
100 g (3½ oz/1 stick less 1 tablespoon) butter
2 tablespoons milk
250 g (9 oz) kadayif shredded pastry (½ packet)
200 g (7 oz/1⅓ cups) pistachios, or a mixture of pistachios and walnuts
200g (7 oz/scant 1 cup) caster (superfine) sugar

Preheat the oven to 180°C (350°F/gas 4). Grease a 20 cm (8 in) square cake tin. Melt the butter with the milk in a small saucepan and set aside to cool slightly.

Gently pull apart the kadayif, making sure none of the strands have clumped together in sticky or dry lumps (discard any bits that are very soggy). Lay it all on a board – it will form an unruly heap – and, using a sharp knife, repeatedly chop straight through the pile, breaking the strands into rough 2.5 cm (1 in) lengths.

Place the chopped kadayif in a bowl and add the melted butter and milk. Using your hands, mix thoroughly, ensuring all the pastry gets a good coating of butter. Divide the buttered kadayif into two equal amounts. Press one half into the bottom of the cake tin, ensuring it completely covers the base. It should be about 2 cm (¾ in) thick.

In a food processor or pestle and mortar, grind the nuts quite finely, to a texture a little coarser than rough sand. Scatter 150 g (5 oz/1 cup) of the nuts over the bottom layer of kadayif pastry, ensuring it is completely covered, right to the edges. Cover the nuts with the second layer of kadayif, pressing it firmly down and to the edges of the tin. Bake in the oven for 1 hour or until the pastry is crisp and lightly golden brown (be careful not to overcook as the nuts may scorch and become bitter, so if over-browning, cover loosely with foil).

Meanwhile put the sugar with 200 ml (7 fl oz/generous ¾ cup) water in a saucepan. Heat gently until dissolved then bring to the boil and boil briskly until the syrup has reduced by a quarter, to about 150 ml (5 fl oz/½ cup). It's

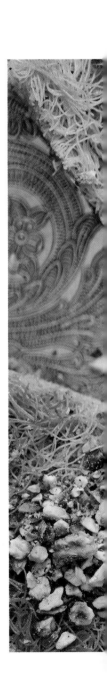

ready when it is viscous and coats the back of a spoon. (Unless it becomes fully syrupy, it won't hold the pastry together.) Remove the syrup from the heat and pour into a jug or bowl to cool.

Remove the Tel Kadayıf from the oven. Pour over the cooled sugar syrup. Leave for 10–15 minutes so the pastry can absorb the syrup and the whole thing can set slightly. Scatter the remaining ground nuts over. Remove from the tin and serve cut into small squares.

Sıcak Helva

Warm Sesame Pudding

Helva is a sweet paste made from sesame seeds and is easy to find in Middle Eastern stores, sold in tubs. It has a distinctive sesame flavour and texture, a little like very thick nougat. The saying in Turkey is that the fish in your stomach will only know that they're dead when you eat some helva and so this is a dessert often sold in fish restaurants. I learned to make it from Olga Tikhonova Irez, a Russian who gave up her corporate career to teach visitors to Istanbul about the city's incredible food culture and who took me on a wonderful food tour of Kadikoy, on the Asian side of the Bosphorus.

SERVES 4–6
450 g (1 lb) plain helva
1 apple, peeled, cored and coarsely grated
finely grated zest and juice of 1 lemon
2 tablespoons milk
¼ teaspoon ground cinnamon
butter/oil for greasing

Preheat the oven to 200°C (400°F/gas 6). Mix the helva, apple, lemon zest and juice together in a bowl and mash with a fork. Add the milk and beat to form a fairly smooth, thick paste.

Pour the helva mixture into a lightly greased, large, shallow ovenproof dish, so that it is no more than 2 cm (¾ in) thick. Sprinkle with the cinnamon and bake for 10 minutes until hot through, then preheat the grill (broiler) to medium.

Place the dish under the grill and allow the top to brown and bubble, watching all the time as it can burn very quickly. Serve immediately.

Fırın Sütlaç

Baked Rice Pudding

In Turkey, rice pudding is a cold dessert and never served hot. Because it needs time to chill, this version – which is halfway between rice pudding and crème brulée – is best made the day before you want to serve it.

SERVES 4

80 g (3 oz/⅓ cup) short-grain pudding rice
700 ml (24 fl oz/2¾ cups) milk
100 g (3½ oz/scant ½ cup) caster (superfine) sugar, plus extra
    for sprinkling
2 drops of natural vanilla extract
65 g (2¼ oz/generous ½ cup) cornflour (cornstarch)

Bring 300 ml (10 fl oz/1¼ cups) water to the boil in a large saucepan and add the rice. Simmer, covered, for 15 minutes, stirring often to prevent sticking (add a splash more water if necessary). When the water has been absorbed by the rice, add the milk, sugar and vanilla extract. Cook for another 15 minutes.

Mix the cornflour with a little water until a smooth loose paste forms. Stir into the pudding mixture. It will quickly thicken. Continue to cook over a low heat, stirring, for 5 minutes. Pour into ramekins or small serving bowls and chill in the fridge until cool and set (about 5 hours or overnight).

Once chilled and set, you can either serve it as it is, sprinkled with cinnamon (in which case it is just called *sütlaç*) or caramelise the top. Preheat the grill (broiler) to medium and lower the rack underneath so the puddings are approximately 15 cm (6 in) from the heat.

Sprinkle each pudding with caster sugar and place under the grill for approximately 5 minutes until the sugar is melted and bubbling and has turned a deep brown (watch carefully as there is a fine line between caramelised and burnt and it can happen very quickly). If you can resist tucking in while they are warm (I often can't) chill again before serving.

Kabak Tatlısı

Baked Pumpkin

In Turkey, pumpkin is very rarely eaten as a savoury dish. Try this method of cooking it for a sweet, wintery dessert. You can cook it with or without the skin – with the skin gives it a distinctive melon-like flavour.

SERVES 4–8
1 small pumpkin, around 1 kg (2 lb 3 oz)
¼ tsp ground cloves or 3 whole ones, ground to a powder
½ teaspoon freshly grated nutmeg
100 g (3½ oz/scant ½ cup) caster (superfine) sugar
vanilla ice cream to serve

Preheat the oven to 200°C (400°F/gas 6). Cut the pumpkin into 8 wedges. Remove the seeds and membranes. Place on a baking sheet, skin-side down, and scatter the spices over each wedge. Pour 3 tablespoons of water into the bottom of the tray. Cover the tray loosely with foil and place in the oven. Bake for 30 minutes, turning the wedges occasionally.

Meanwhile make a sugar syrup by heating 100 ml (3½ fl oz/generous ⅓ cup) water and the sugar, stirring until the sugar dissolves. Then bring to the boil and simmer for 5 minutes.

When the pumpkin has been in the oven for 30 minutes, lay the wedges on their sides and pour the syrup over. Cook for a further 5 minutes, then set the wedges skin-side down again. Cook for 10 minutes more, then check the flesh is soft. Serve hot with vanilla ice cream.

Havuçlu Kek

Carrot Cake

Cakes are much loved in Istanbul and patisseries dot the city, selling anything from gaudily decorated, brightly coloured towers with multiple tiers,
to simple treats full of spices and nuts. One afternoon – while trying to find
the famous market in Beşiktaş – I bought a couple of wedges of carrot cake
to keep me going. This is my version and it always takes me back to that hot
afternoon (the market was worth seeking out, too).

MAKES ONE CAKE
200 g (7 oz/1¾ cups) plain (all-purpose) flour
½ teaspoon salt
2 teaspoons baking powder
½ teaspoon freshly grated nutmeg
1 teaspoon ground cinnamon
3 tablespoons ground almonds
3 eggs
150 g (5 oz/⅔ cup) caster (superfine) sugar
150 ml (5 fl oz/⅔ cup) vegetable oil
175 g (6 oz/generous cup) finely grated carrot
75 g (2½ oz/½ cup) currants, soaked in boiling water for 10 minutes
60 g (2 oz/½ cup) roughly chopped walnuts
finely grated zest of 1½ lemons
icing (confectioners') sugar to dust (optional)
5-6 tablespoons plain Turkish or Greek-style yoghurt to serve

Grease an 18 cm/7 in springform cake tin. Preheat the oven to 180°C
(350°F/gas 4). Sift the flour, salt, baking powder, nutmeg and cinnamon
together and stir in the ground almonds.

Mix the eggs, sugar and oil together in a bowl and whisk vigorously until
foamy and doubled in volume.

Add the carrot, currants, walnuts and the zest of 1 lemon and stir gently.
Then, fold in the sifted dry ingredients.

Pour the batter into the cake tin and bake for 50 minutes until the cake is
golden on top, shrinking slightly from the edges of the tin and the centre
springs back when lightly pressed. Remove from the oven and cool in the
tin for 30 minutes, then turn out onto a wire rack to cool completely. Dust
the top with icing sugar, if using. Mix most of the remaining zest with
yoghurt, keeping a little back to garnish and serve with the cake. Sprinkle
the last of the zest over the yoghurt.

Revani

Semolina Cake

This dense, sweet cake benefits hugely from being made the day before
you want to eat it, allowing the semolina to soak up the syrup and soften.
There is any number of variations from across the country and surrounding
regions – some stud the top with almonds, others sprinkle it with pistachios. You can also make it with orange blossom water or grated coconut.
I like to serve it with fresh berries as their tartness cuts through the sweetness of the cake. A slice is a lovely foil to a short, strong cup of rich Turkish
coffee, or a cup of black tea.

MAKES 1 CAKE
For the syrup:
250 g (9 oz/generous 1 cup) caster (superfine) sugar
juice of ½ lemon
berries and a little honey to serve

For the cake:
5 eggs, separated
125 g (4 oz/½ cup) caster (superfine) sugar
150 g (5 oz/⅔ cup) butter, melted, and cooled
2 heaped tablespoons plain Turkish or Greek-style yoghurt
finely grated zest of 1 lemon
150 g (5 oz/1¼ cups) fine semolina (cream of wheat)
110 g (3¾ oz/scant 1 cup) plain (all-purpose) flour
1 tablespoon baking powder

Preheat the oven to 180°C (350°F/gas 4). Line a 20 cm (8 in) square cake tin
with baking paper. Mix the sugar for the syrup with 250 ml (8½ fl oz/1 cup)
water in a saucepan and heat, stirring until the sugar dissolves. Bring to
the boil and boil for around 10 minutes until reduced and syrupy. Stir in the
lemon juice. Leave to cool before using.

   Whisk the egg whites until stiff. Whisk the egg yolks and sugar together
until thick and pale and the whisk leaves a trail when lifted out of the
mixture.

   Slowly add the cooled melted butter, whisking all the time. Add the
yoghurt, lemon zest and semolina, and mix thoroughly. Sift the flour and
baking powder together then gently fold into the mixture with a metal
spoon. Finally fold in the egg whites, taking care to knock out as little of
the air as possible.

Turn the mixture into the prepared tin. Bake for 30 minutes, then check the cake. If the top is browning too fast, lower the heat by 10 degrees or so. Cook for another 10 minutes, and then check again. The cake is cooked when it has risen, is golden brown and the centre springs back when lightly pressed.

Remove from the oven. With the cake still in the tin, cut it into diamond shaped pieces and pour over the cooled syrup. Allow the cake to absorb the syrup for at least 4 hours, and preferably overnight. Remove from the tin and serve with fresh berries. For extra indulgence, drizzle with a little clear honey.

Ayran

Salted Yoghurt Drink

Ayran is a light, seriously refreshing, slightly salted yoghurt drink, a little bit like Indian lassi. It is drunk with everything and at all times of day, particularly with meals in restaurants where alcohol isn't served. For extra coolness, add a few ice cubes to the blender.

MAKES 2 GLASSES
240 ml (8 fl oz/scant 1 cup) plain Turkish or Greek-style yoghurt
240 ml (8 fl oz/1 cup) well-chilled water
½ teaspoon salt, or to taste

Pour the yoghurt and water in a blender and season with the salt. Blitz until foamy. Pour into chilled glasses and serve. Alternatively, whisk the ingredients together with an electric or balloon whisk.

Karpuz ve Zencefil Suyu

Watermelon and Ginger Juice

A refreshing drink with a little kick, this is perfect for a hot summer day. Watermelon juice makes a great base for cocktails too – just add a shot of vodka or rum.

MAKES ABOUT 4 GLASSES
½ watermelon, chilled in the fridge
5 cm (2 in) piece of fresh ginger, peeled
ice cubes to serve (optional)

Deseed the melon, remove the rind and chop into chunks. Blitz in a blender. Slice the ginger into strips and crush lightly in a pestle and mortar or with a rolling pin. Add to the watermelon pulp, including any ginger juice, and stand for 10 minutes.

Using a sieve and pressing through with the back of a spoon, if necessary, strain the juice into glasses and add ice, if you like.

Limonata

Lemonade

On a hot day, a jug of this lemonade syrup, ready to be diluted with cool water, is the perfect thing to have in the fridge. It will keep, sealed, for about a week in the fridge.

MAKES 6 GLASSES
finely grated zest and juice of 6 unwaxed lemons
200 g (7 oz/scant 1 cup) caster (superfine) sugar
still or sparkling water and ice cubes to serve
mint sprigs to garnish

Put the lemon zest and juice and the sugar in a saucepan with 450 ml (15 fl oz/2 cups) water. Stir well. Bring slowly to the boil. Simmer for a minute or two and stir to ensure the sugar dissolves completely.

Remove from the heat and allow to cool. Strain into a clean bottle and store in the fridge. Dilute 40:60 with chilled still or sparkling water, or to taste. Garnish with mint sprigs and serve with lots of ice.

REBECCA SEAL is a food and drink writer. Previously she worked at *Observer Food Monthly* and is now freelance, writing for newspapers such as the *Financial Times* and magazines such as *Grazia*, as well as making frequent appearances on Channel 4. She lives in London with her partner, photographer Steven Joyce.

STEVEN JOYCE is a photographer specialising in food, travel and portraiture. His work regularly features in national newspapers, magazines and recipe books.

Acknowledgements

Thanks to the writer Ansel Mullins for giving us his time, knowledge of Istanbul and a copy of his terrific food guidebook to the city, *Istanbul Eats* (his brilliant blog is at www.instanbuleats.com); Arzu Gürdamar for rushing back from a holiday in Greece to meet us, show us cookbooks and feed us at her wonderful restaurant, Dai Pera (www.dairestaurant.com); chef Didem Şenol from restaurant Lokanta Maya (www.lokantamaya.com) and cafe Gram (www.grampera.com), for taking the time to talk to us about the iconic dishes of Istanbul, giving us her gorgeous book *Flavours of the Aegean* and for letting us use her famous courgette fritter recipe; chef Gencay Ucok for making us very full and not a little tipsy at his amazing restaurant Meze by Lemon Tree (www.mezze.com.tr) and for a food tour of Istanbul that took in corners of the city we would never have found without him, including that tripe soup...; Olga Tikhonova Irez for taking us on a Delicious Istanbul walking tour of Kadıköy market and then teaching us how to cook our finds (www.deliciousistanbul.com); Metin Gursoy and his friend the artist Emel Kurhan for sharing some of their favourite foodie places in Istanbul and giving me a copy of her beautiful book, *Emel Loves Istanbul*; Marti Hotel in Taksim for spoiling us with a luxurious five-star break, letting us use their beef kofte recipe and teaching us the ways of Turkish rice pudding (www.martiistanbulhotel.com); and huge thanks to Hulya Solyu at Redmint Communications who worked with the Turkish Tourism Office to help get us back to Istanbul time and again. Thanks to all at Hardie Grant: Stephen King, Kate Pollard, Kajal Mistry and Caroline Brown, it's been a real pleasure working with you, and to Clare Skeats for her beautiful design. Eleanor Millington lent me her baking know-how and Erdem Kayalar kindly helped me with Turkish spellings and meanings (any mistakes that remain are all mine though). Thank you to Steven Joyce, for his beautiful photographs of course, but also for creating this book with me, from beginning to end.

Teşekkür Ederim to you all.

Istanbul 2013 by Rebecca Seal and Steven Joyce

First published in 2013 by Hardie Grant Books

Hardie Grant Books London
Dudley House, North Suite
34–35 Southampton Street
London WC2E 7HF
www.hardiegrant.co.uk

Hardie Grant Books (Australia)
Ground Floor, Building 1
658 Church Street
Melbourne, VIC 3121
www.hardiegrant.com.au

British Library Cataloguing-in-Publication Data.
A catalogue record for this book is available from the British Library.

ISBN 978-1-74270-601-6

Commissioning Editor: Kate Pollard

Desk Editor: Kajal Mistry

Cover and Internal design: Clare Skeats

Photography and retouching: Steven Joyce

Pattern on cover and pages 16–17, 36–37, 58–59, 118–119, 180–181, 206–207, 218–219:
rendered by Anna Salmane, taken from *Islamic Geometric Patterns* by Eric Broug,
published by Thames & Hudson 2008. Every attempt has been made to contact the
copyright holders. The publishers would like to hear from any copyright holder who
may not have been attributed.

Colour reproduction by p2D

Printed and bound China by 1010 Printing International Limited

10 9 8 7 6 5 4 3 2 1